Markets

Economy and Society

Markets

Patrik Aspers

polity

First published in 2011 by Polity Press

Polity Press
65 Bridge Street
Cambridge CB2 1UR, UK

Polity Press
350 Main Street
Malden, MA 02148, USA

ISBN-13: 978-0-7456-4577-3
ISBN-13: 978-0-7456-4578-0(pb)

A catalogue record for this book is available from the British Library.

Typeset in 11 on 13 pt Sabon
by Servis Filmsetting Ltd, Stockport, Cheshire
Printed and bound in Great Britain by MPG Books Group Limited, Bodmin, Cornwall

For further information on Polity, visit our website: www.politybooks.com

Contents

Contents

Contents

Figures and Tables

Figures

Tables

Preface

We all regularly participate in markets. We do it when filling up the car with gasoline, when buying a bagel on the way to a lecture, or when deciding which book to buy from the Internet bookstore. Markets have become taken for granted, and they are so integrated in our daily activities that we can hardly act without participating in them. But as people come face to face with economic reality, not least due to the financial crisis that began in 2007 and continued to unfold to the date of finalizing this book, they have increasingly become aware of how markets can fail and cause turmoil, but also that they are globally interconnected. In other words, people, regardless of whether they wish to be or not, are affected by the global market economy.

Although neither markets nor research on markets are recent phenomena, it is clear that markets have attracted more interest in the public debate, as well as in the research community, over the past 20 years. The field of "new economic sociology" came into being in the mid-1980s in the USA, and markets soon became one of its central fields of research. The wave of conservative politics with a liberal market view associated in the USA above all with Republican President Ronald Reagan, who held office from 1981 to 1989, and Margaret Thatcher, British Prime Minister from 1979 to 1990, has certainly affected the centrality of markets in the public debate. What we call globalization is partly marketization at the global level, but also the rise of truly global markets.

Preface

This book aims to introduce and discuss the burgeoning research on markets that social scientists have produced, with a focus on the sociological contribution. It offers a systematic overview of the central issues in the academic discussion of markets, with the ambition of giving readers enough detail to understand and to conduct analyses of real markets.

We face markets on a daily basis, but the everyday concepts we use to describe them – for example, consumer markets, producer markets, business-to-business markets, or labor, financial, global, consumer, and monopoly "markets" – may not be the most useful ones if we want to understand and explain what goes on in markets. These different market prefixes have been created on an ad hoc basis, but what we need are ways of making theoretically grounded distinctions between types of markets. Thus, what kinds of markets can be observed and what distinctions should be made are central questions. What we also want to know is how markets are interrelated, and how they affect each other. Moreover, the conditions and consequences of markets are discussed in the literature, but what is lacking is a clear understanding of what is general to all markets, and what is specific to the various concrete markets we experience and observe.

This book's ambition is not only to review the existing literature, but to offer a sociological approach to markets. It aims to make a number of specific contributions. The first contribution is to generate systematic and analytic knowledge of markets. The second is to provide an approach to understanding and explaining markets.

Having a systematic and analytical knowledge of markets is also the condition for contributing to the broader societal discussion of "market society" and capitalism. Seen from an analytical point of view, it is almost paradoxical that so much has been written on market society and capitalism without defining or paying enough attention, theoretically or empirically, to its most central institutions, markets.

A central argument of this book is that we should talk about markets instead of *the* market. In social life, we face concrete markets, but "the market," as in the "Single Market" of the EU, is nowhere to be found. To make this point clear, we must show what markets are and how different markets work. This book provides a definition that encompasses all markets: a market is a social structure for the exchange of rights in which offers are evaluated and priced, and compete with one another.

At a more general level, I stress in this book that markets should be understood as a basic form of coordination. This is to follow the path of Simmel, identifying social units and forms of relations that can be observed in several social spheres. To view markets as a form of economic coordination suggests that we can compare markets with other forms of economic coordination, notably hierarchies (organizations) and networks.

A central claim of the book is that economic actions are essentially social, which has consequences for the definition of the economy. I see it as central to replace economic man with social human man, instead of trying to add flesh and blood to economic man, as so many social scientists have tried to do.

The book identifies a number of central ideas which have sometimes been accommodated and taken for granted in contemporary texts on markets. I will thus focus on the arguments and the original sources, and then relate them to more contemporary thinkers, instead of merely reviewing the existing literature. This is an attempt to reduce complexity by presenting the most central ideas without being caught up in the details. Details will not be spared when they are needed to explain and discuss important issues, however.

This book offers a map which can help to sort different approaches in accordance with the form of markets, rather than according to the more traditional dividing lines in economic sociology, such as cultural, structural (network), or organizational perspectives.

To accomplish its aim, the book uses and presents a substantial portion of the research on markets which has been done in the social sciences. But it provides a particular perspective on the material. Although this is the task and responsibility of the author, no author is an island; "I" is henceforth replaced by "we."

Acknowledgments

The bulk of this book has been written at the Max Planck Institute for the Study of Societies in Cologne, Germany. Other parts were written in Sweden, where I am based as a researcher at the Department of Sociology and SCORE at Stockholm University.

Regardless of how many books an academic has written, any interpretation is grounded in her lifeworld. Our knowledge of markets is conditioned by us taking part in markets on a daily basis. This, however, is not enough to gain the academic view on reality. What I know, and the value of this is to be judged by you as a reader, I have learned from reading texts and from talking to colleagues all over the world. The research group on markets at the Max Planck Institute for the Study of Societies in Cologne has been the most natural arena for discussions. The research group was set up in 2005, and I was there from the start. This group, and the work we have done, has been an important resource for the results presented here. In discussion with many of its members, Jens Beckert, Philipp Gerlach, Thorsten Kogge, Mark Lutter, Guido Möllering, Sascha Münich, Geny Piotti, Irene Troy, Raymund Werle, and Frank Wehinger, central questions of this book have been developed. A graduate seminar at the Oslo Summer School (at Oslo University) in 2008 was instructive to the formation of important ideas for this book, and so too were comments from Risto Heiskala.

Alexander Dobeson has provided valuable input for the historical part of the book. Sebastian Kohl has been involved in

Acknowledgments

the research on several of the matters discussed. The anonymous reviewers and my editors at Polity Press, Jonathan Skerrett and Emma Longstaff, as well as Helen Gray, the copy-editor, have helped me to improve the quality of this work.

My work with the book has benefited from financial support from the Max Planck Institute for the Study of Societies, Stockholm University – the Department of Sociology and SCORE, with the research grant on Organization of Markets (M2007-0244:1-PK) from the Riksbankens Jubileumsfond – and the research grant (2009-1958) from the Swedish Research Council (VR).

That the topic of markets is pivotal in economic sociology was shown to me by Richard Swedberg. What he has given can never be returned, only passed on. I dedicate this book to Richard, my dear friend and teacher.

The final revision of this book has been done in a small village on the east coast of Sweden, where the social and economic importance of other forms of economic coordination, too, are more clearly seen.

Patrik Aspers, Axmarby, June 20, 2010

1

Introduction

When people are surveyed on how much alcohol they have consumed during the past week, they commonly underestimate their consumption. This they do not because of the direct effects of alcohol, but because they tend to forget some of the occasions when it was consumed, as they form part of their daily lives. If you were asked how many markets you have been involved in over the past week, could you give the correct answer? This depends on what we mean by "market," but we can agree that there are many, and it is likely that you would leave out a few of them.

Although markets have not existed since the dawn of humankind, and much of social life takes place outside markets, few will have failed to notice that markets have become central in our everyday lives. If you are living in the UK, Germany, China, or the USA, you, and your activities, are embedded in markets. Children are born into a lifeworld in which markets are taken for granted. It does not take long before they start to play "shop." Markets have over time penetrated other areas of life, as is manifested by the introduction of life insurance and its accompanying markets. This penetration of market activities into various spheres of our lives means that we have the opportunity to make a choice, but it also means that we *have* to make choices. Markets have created wealth but they are also part of the reasons for the emergence of economic crises. Let us begin by looking at how markets are related to one another.

Markets not Market

Markets do not come in isolation, but together. The reason is that markets are embedded in one another. Let us take one particular consumer market that we all know as our point of departure and see where it leads us. When you buy a pair of trousers in a local store, the firm from which you buy the pair of trousers competes with other fashion stores by offering different price and fashion/quality levels. The money you use for the purchase is transferred from you to the firm selling the garment, perhaps using a credit or debit card. The card is issued by a bank, and banks compete with other banks to have customers' savings and deposit accounts, but they also compete with each other for the capital they need to lend to customers and firms. The bank holds money, which is issued by the state – money which is traded in currency markets, around the clock, all over the world. The plastic card is issued by a company that competes with others to offer its services to banks. Firms that employ labor need capital to get off the ground, to invest, and to give credit, and to obtain capital they may take part in different investment markets. Furthermore, production of garments is today a global affair, largely coordinated in markets, populated by buying firms in some countries and suppliers in others, with much lower cost of labor.

Although it is possible, no firm controls the entire garment production chain, which also includes, for example, food for the workers and many other suppliers who may not be directly involved in the production of the garments. The relationship between the fashion firm and its suppliers who manufacture the trousers is established across a market, and it is typical in this market that buyers are located in developed countries, and manufacturers are spread across the globe in less developed countries. The competitors that a manufacturer in India faces can be firms in the same industrial district, but it could also be producers in China or Mexico.

The manufacturing supplier operates in several markets. It buys input material, such as zippers and fabrics, from firms or agents of firms in different markets. The goods have to be shipped and insured, which involves actors who operate in yet other markets. The fashion firm and its suppliers operate in different labor markets. Some of these may be global and others extremely local, and in some stages of production – for example, among suppliers of the garment manufacturers, or even among the suppliers' suppliers – we can be almost certain that the economy touches on "informal" or "black" markets. The firm that washes the garments before they are shipped may, for example, have suppliers who employ illegal immigrants.

The questions to be addressed

We experience the "market economy" directly and indirectly on a daily basis. Its complexity, however, is often hidden in the wheels within wheels of relations between markets, hierarchies, and networks. A whole range of concrete questions must be addressed if we are to better understand and explain this complexity. For example, how come sellers (and buyers) on the stock exchange are anonymous, whereas sellers in a consumer mass market are known as brands? How is it that markets rather than the activities of peddlers or fairs have become the dominant form of exchange? Can one have capitalism without markets? What are the conditions for black markets? How come some objects are traded in markets and not others?

There are also a number of more theoretical questions which researchers must pose if we are to understand markets. How is order achieved in markets? What roles do the offers, social structure, and culture of the market play with regard to order in the market? Where do markets end? What other forms of economic coordination are possible as alternatives to the market? The overarching question is as trite as it is tricky: what is a market? We shall now attempt to provide a definition, upon which the rest of the book will rest.

Market Definition

This and the following section will deal with the core of markets and, although they are dense, we will continue to discuss these central issues at length and in detail in the chapters to come. A *market* is a social structure for the exchange of rights in which offers are evaluated and priced, and compete with one another, which is shorthand for the fact that actors – individuals and firms – compete with one another via offers. This definition covers the market as a place, as well as markets as an "institution." This connection is observed not only if we trace the phenomenon – as we shall do in chapter 3 – but also in its Latin etymology, *mercatus*, which refers to trade, but also to place. Another notion, *forum*, should also be mentioned. It refers more specifically to place and market place. Both, however, refer to public activities. Each market usually has a name, which normally refers to what is being traded – for example, the market for military aircraft – but, as we will see, the product is not necessarily the ordering principle of the market. Other markets, and their names, are connected to a specific place, such as Spitalfields market in London.

Like other definitions, this market definition is based on the lifeworld and its bed of taken-for-granted behavior, institutions, and propositions which represent and enable all kinds of social relations. What we shall concentrate on, however, is, as a first step, the essential market elements that constitute the definition. Only then shall we look at the three equally necessary prerequisites which, in contrast to the elements of the definition, may be solved in different ways. When the definition and the market prerequisites are taken together, we have a good view of what makes markets different from other social formations.

Elements of the market definition

The rest of the book assumes that structures are the result of human activities which have become "coagulated," so that they are, in relative terms, stable over time. Fundamentally, we can talk of a structure because of actors' shared practices and/or cognitive frames. The notion of structure thus accounts for the fact that a market has extension over time. The market structure is constituted by the two roles, buyer and seller, each standing on one side of the market, facing the other. This means that a market implies a record of actual transactions and not merely potential transactions. The two roles have different interests (Swedberg 2004): "to sell at a high price" and to "buy at a low price" (Geertz 1992: 226). It is only because of actors' interest in trading that there can be a market (Swedberg 2003). In a market, actors get something in return for what they give up; this is the generic buy-and-sell relationship. A market is characterized by "voluntary" and peaceful interaction (Weber 1922: 383; 1968: 17), and this follows from the fact that property rights – that is, a form of ownership based on socially recognized economic rights (Carruthers and Ariovich 2004: 30) that fixate the underlying assets – are accepted. The property rights that actors exchange must be recognized; if not, we must either speak of robbery, if one party simply takes everything, or gift giving, if one party gives without getting anything in return. Property rights, moreover, must be possible to enforce in all kinds of trading, not just market trading, and this facilitates trade (North 1990).[1]

To accept property rights is not to deny the struggle (Simmel 1923: 216–32; Weber 1978) inherent in the processes of "higgling and bargaining" (Marshall 1961: 453) between buyers and sellers (Swedberg 1998) in the market, and rivalry between actors on the same side (Simmel 1955: 57). Pure market transactions have a distinct ending, in contrast, for example, to the openness and future orientation of network relations (Powell 1990). Market exchange is a voluntary form of economic coordination in which actors have a choice: they can decide to trade, sell, or buy whatever is seen as a legitimate offer, at the price at which they are offered, but they do not have to. In the past, when one slave owner sold slaves on the market to other slave owners, this – as appalling as it may seem – was as much a market as when children choose which lollipop to buy in the supermarket. As long as the property rights and the right to trade are legitimate, granted by the state or any other force capable of imposing sanctions, if only among those who control the rights, a market can exist. Property rights, of course, are also enforced by means of violence, reputation and status in illegal markets, for example, those controlled by the Mafia (Gambetta 1996). Property rights are often embedded in social custom, which means that they are normally not contested (Hodgson 1988: 147–71).

With the help of these notions, let us now try to see what falls outside of market interaction. People may be more or less forced to sell goods, and even their organs or children, in a market. This does not necessarily affect the way the market functions. The issue at stake is how illegal and/or immoral actions push (by force) and pull (through the expected "prosperity") people and their goods into a market, not the question of whether it is a market or not. However, the capturing of slaves in Africa or elsewhere was not a market, as the slaves did not have a choice. That the slave market is characterized by voluntary transactions by the owners of the assets – the slaves – does not mean that participation in the market is a joyful experience for those being traded. In other markets, too, people are sold, for example, players who are traded from one club to another in the National Hockey League or in European soccer. However, these players get a large sum of the costs of transfer, and they decided to be on this market, and seem to know the conditions.

We must, consequently, separate the question of how the offers in the market are made from analysis of the market. As indicated, the objects of trade in markets must not only be of interest to the actors, but must also be morally legitimate objects of market transactions, as Zelizer and others have shown (Zelizer 1979, 1981; Healy 2006). Some objects of trade are "blocked" from being exchanged, such as political decisions (Beckert 2006). Financial markets which, by and large, are seen as legitimate today, have only gradually become so; they were not necessarily legitimate outside financial circles in the eighteenth century, when "financial transactions took place in coffee houses and in the adjacent streets, with traders and customers often chased by the police" (Preda 2009: 60–1). Legitimacy must be separated from the distinction between legal and illegal markets; the market for student apartments in the former Soviet Union was seen by many as morally legitimate, though it was illegal (Katsenelinboigen 1977). Legitimacy as a market condition may appear as tautological, but the important point is to think of the degree of legitimacy a certain market has – some black markets are, under certain conditions, accepted by many, and in other cases by few people; an issue to which we return in chapter 7, which deals with the making of markets. We may conclude that the market as a form of coordination does not, per se, exclude trade of any kind of goods or services. We can thus observe "black" or illegal markets, meaning trade of objects that are not legal to trade.

Trade and markets

All exchange in markets is trade, but not all trade takes place in markets. In contrast to trade, which can take place between two parties who exchange different kinds of "rights," markets are characterized by two additional elements, interchangeability of the roles of buyers and sellers, and competition.[2] Roles imply the exchangeability of sellers and buyers. Consequently, in a market, in contrast to trade, at least one of the two sides, whether the buying or the selling side, must be composed of at least two actors. Thus, the minimum number of actors required for a market to exist is three; only with three actors can we talk of roles. This is the condition for a comparison of their offers. Comparison is not enough to have a market, however. To speak of a market, as the definition suggests, requires that there is competition between at least two offers (parties), on the one side, for exchange with the other side. It is in this selection process that evaluation takes place in such a way that competing offers can be compared to each other. Competition refers to the relation between two or more actors aiming for an end that cannot be shared between them.[3] It must be underlined that competition is for the benefit of the third party, who enjoys the advantages derived from it – *tertius gaudens*. It is this actor, for example, a single buyer, who can choose among those who strive to sell their offers, who benefits from the competition, not those who compete (Simmel 1955: 154–62). Figure 1.1 illustrates the distinction between trade and market.

The difference between trade and market, both of which are instances of economic exchange, suggests that the connotation,

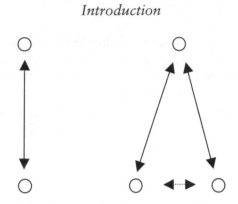

Figure 1.1 Trade and market relations as two forms of economic exchange.

Note: The arrows represent relations between actors, who are depicted as circles.

already mentioned, of the market as something "public," or transparent, is important. Competition can be either public or secret. The *tertius gaudens* buyer may utilize its superior position and let two or more sellers compete publicly so that participants and others know of this, but this may also be secret so that no actor but *tertius gaudens* is aware of the competition that takes place among the sellers. Moreover, if one side – for example, a single seller – lies to the only existing buyer that there is also another buyer, we have "quasi-competition" since this may cause the only buyer to reveal how much value he would be willing to give the product in a "real" competition. In some cases, we have competition among both sellers and buyers in a market; this is the case in the so-called double auction of stock exchanges.

Public prices are of considerable importance for making markets transparent, and the fact that markets generate transparency is an important aspect by means of which they operate as coordination devices. Competition must not boil down to price competition between homogeneous goods – this is just one special case. Competition can be due to innovation, as in Schumpeterian economics (Nelson 2005: 9), or to virtually any variables which are identifiable with regard to the offer, such as quality, service, or style (Chamberlin 1953).

Prerequisites of Market Order

We have now outlined what a market is by describing its essential characteristics. There are, in addition, three prerequisites that must be met for a market to be ordered; in other words, so that we can talk of a market. We have decided to treat them separately, as each of them can be met in empirically different ways: either actively, such as by organized coordination, or passively, in the form of an emergent order. The first prerequisite is that it is clear what is traded in the market; the second is that there must be rules governing what to do and what not to do in the market, and, finally, the offers of what is traded must obtain an economic value in the market. These will be discussed in detail in chapter 4.

1. *What the market is "about."* Human organs are not sold in the same market as cars. Garments are sold in yet another market. This means that "things" that are acknowledged as similar are traded in the "same" market.
2. *How things are done in the market.* The second prerequisite has to do with culture in the market. We define culture as beliefs, norms, "tools," rules and behaviors – for example, discourse and practice – appropriate to the setting. That is to say that the institutional framework may differ, including between markets that "are about the same thing," such as two different markets in which the shares of one company is traded.
3. *The value of the offer.* Given that actors know what is traded, the economic value of the good can, and must, be determined. This can be done in different ways, for example, in different forms of auctions (Smith 1989), or in markets such as food stores, in which the sellers offer groceries with fixed prices; consumers can then react to these prices.

When the elements described are present, and the prerequisites are met, we have an ordered market. It is only when there is order that we can talk of a market. The order enables actors to overcome uncertainty (Beckert 1996; White 2002b: 1). However, in any existing market the problem of order has already been solved (Luhmann 1981). In fact, the question of order is central to both sociologists (for example, Aspers 2010; Beckert 2009b) and economists (Nelson and Winter 2002: 23). One difference is that sociologists focus on order as a result of value or of social structure, and refer to, for example, moral order (Durkheim 1984), whereas economists focus on equilibria, which emerge in evolutionary processes (Nelson and Winter 2002). From a sociological point of view, the problem of order is the fundamental problem, which of course means that it is central also in the economy. Equilibrium is only one form of how order is made, as will be shown, and this suggests that the sociological question is more profound than the economic question. The latter is more narrowly defined and it comes with a full set of assumptions, including, for example, many small actors, homogeneous products, free entry and exit.

Summary and Outline of the Book

The first chapter summarizes the various theoretical concepts which will be discussed in more detail in later chapters. A market definition is the starting point of any serious discussion of markets, and it is upon this idea of market, and the corresponding idea of identities in markets, that we will build throughout the rest of the book. In the following chapters we shall present the sociological foundations and starting point for the economy and, more explicitly, the sociology of markets.

Each chapter begins with an introduction that ties it to the previous chapter(s) and ends with a summary. At the end of the book, we present our findings and suggest a set of questions to pose when studying markets, as well as additional areas of research.

In chapter 2, we draw on the definitions drawn and look at the general economic problem of production and consumption under the condition of uncertainty, to see how it can be solved by different coordination forms: markets, networks, and hierarchies. This analysis contrasts markets with other forms of economic coordination, thereby clarifying what they are and what they are not. Chapter 2 also deals with the expansion of markets at the expense of other forms of economic coordination. Chapter 3 takes a closer look at the actors who populate markets and also puts markets in the larger social context, with a discussion of the history of markets and market society. The fourth chapter makes several important distinctions that pertain to markets. The most important addresses the roots of market order. Order can be rooted in either offers or the social structure, although real markets are usually the result of a combination. Chapter 4 presents central ideas of man as the foundation for market theories, introduces the distinction between status and standard markets, between switch-role and fixed-role markets; this chapter also discusses monopoly markets and other forms. In this discussion, the most important kinds of markets are clarified. Chapters 5 and 6 provide ample discussion of markets, based upon the distinctions made in chapter 4. In chapter 5, we study markets in which the offers traded in the market are entrenched; these markets are called standard markets, and it is among such markets that we classify the neoclassical market model. Chapter 6 mirrors chapter 5, but focuses on markets in which the specific social structure is more entrenched than the offers in the market. To analyze how markets are made is the task of chapter 7. The last chapter of the book, chapter 8, concludes, but also looks ahead and discusses areas of research, as well as methods with which to research markets.

2

Coordination in the Economy

The first problem for human beings was not how to act in a market, but survival. To survive, our predecessors had to gather, hunt, produce offspring, build shelter, and, more generally, to protect themselves from the environment, as well as learn how to extract resources from it. They started to cultivate the environment to serve their purposes. This cultivation, of course, includes human beings and social life. Historical, sociological, and anthropological research has provided ample information on cultural variation, in the broadest sense of the word. Regardless of what historical path we follow, it took much effort and time before the first "markets" with any similarity to what we observe today were made.

The discussion of the historical development of markets is postponed until chapter 3, while here we continue to develop the tools for understanding and explaining markets. This chapter focuses on forms of economic coordination, that is, forms of bringing people and resources together in an orderly fashion to enable production, consumption, and distribution. In addition to markets as a form of economic coordination, there are hierarchies, which are often seen as organizations, networks, and autarchies. By contrasting markets to other social formations, it will be easier to understand what markets are and what they are not. First, we analyze the economy and define the most central economic problem. Then we discuss the different forms of economic coordination in addition to markets, followed by a discussion of how these ideal-typical forms are related to each other, also in the real economy.

The Economy

We have said that markets reside in the economy, but left the notion of "economy" undefined. It is embarrassing that new economic sociology has not generated a definition of the economy, as pointed out by Sklair (1997). To do this, we first turn to some existing definitions. Economy refers, in its etymological sense, to the administration of a household, a farm, or an enterprise; one definition of the economy goes back to Aristotle – or, more correctly, Xenophon. Xenophon wrote the text in the fourth century BC for the purpose of the "gentleman landowners," who were the citizens. Xenophon's text is a set of instructions on how to manage the household, and it refers to how to have a good life, how to treat and organize one's wife and slaves, and the technology of farming (Xenophon 1970). This notion of the economy is clearly broader than the one we use today.

Xenophon's concepts reflected the situation at the time, and the definition that economist Alfred Marshall proposed, about two thousand years later, is similar in this respect:

> Political Economy or Economics is a study of mankind in the ordinary business of life; it examines that part of individual and social action which is most closely connected with the attainment and with the use of the material requisites of wellbeing. Thus it is on the one side a study of wealth; and on the other, and more important side, a part of the study of man. (Marshall 1961: 1)

Marshall's broad definition puts humanity and, indirectly, social life, at the center of the economy, and it refers to the production, distribution, and consumption of wealth. Wealth refers not only to material conditions, as its etymology includes being "happy" and "prosperous."[1] Nonetheless, it has somehow to be "produced." How and what to *produce*, a notion which refers to something that is done or generated, was the first concrete problem facing humanity. Human beings have made progress over several thousand years, and one consequence is that the importance of consumption has gradually increased. Marshall, who follows Aristotle and Marx, viewed activities ("production") as more important than wants ("consumption"): "[A]lthough it is man's wants in the earliest stages of his development that give rise to his activities, yet afterwards each new step upward is to be regarded as the development of new activities giving rise to new wants, rather than of new wants giving rise to new activities" (Marshall 1961: 89). "Want" has its roots in Scandinavian languages (*vänta*) and means to wait for something that is missing and that is not there yet. The active solution is to "produce" what we want (are waiting for). Thus, wants (consumption), or what we are missing, are tied to our activities (production).

However, many economists, at least since Lionel Robbins's work in 1932, define economics not as the study of a specific entity, the economy, but as an approach to understanding social life from a certain point of view: "Economics is the science which studies human behavior as a relationship between ends and scarce means which have alternative uses" (Robbins 1935: 16). Another economist, Hayek, follows this idea, declaring that an economy "consists of a complex of activities by which a given set of means is allocated in accordance with a unitary plan among competing ends according to their relative importance" (Hayek 1976: 107). Hayek's formal definition of the economy is in line with the Austrian school of economics, of which he was part, and includes those activities that are valued due to their importance, thus stressing "scarcity" in relation to what actors want (Menger 1994: 77). The action theory at the heart of economics is a decision theory on how to act that has been turned into an assumption of how real actors behave. These formal definitions say more about the imperialist ambitions of economics (Stigler 1982) than about what the economy is, or its "substance."

Furthermore, actors in economics are isolated atoms who try to maximize their utility. In fact, the economic definition of the "Robinson Crusoe economy" developed by economists means that "Economic character is by no means restricted to goods that are the objects of human economy in a social context" (Menger 1994: 77). However, the perfect "economic laboratory" of the stranded Crusoe dismisses what cannot be left out – Crusoe is essentially social in his orientation and cannot become non-social.

Coordination in the Economy

What then is the economy? We rely on the following definition of the *economy*: people's coordination of production, consumption, and distribution of wealth. Economic sociology is the study of this. This implies that the economy is inherently social and that actors' orientation to others (Swedberg 1999; Weber 1978) is of central importance when addressing economic issues too. Economic theory – as we will see in chapter 3 – is merely one approach on the economy that restricts the assumption on humanity.

It is, moreover, worth stressing how this definition implies a radically different view from what is normal in economic sociology – the application of the sociological approach to the study of the economy. This unfortunate definition simply involves "the social" being added to "the economic." Economic sociology, in other words, took over the economic view of humanity, economy, and economic action from the outset. Moreover, as many sociologists have taken over questions from economics, such as equilibrium and the idea of what a market is, essentially without questioning them or their foundations, history, or etymology, the sociological contribution to our understanding of the economy has not yet fulfilled its potential. Economic sociology has so far taken upon its shoulders the responsibility of rectifying this, by adding flesh and blood to "economic man," as he is called in economics.[2]

Our definition, which draws on social human beings, stresses, in contrast, the essentially social starting point of economic activities. This definition also implies that all spheres of life may include social economic activities or consequences for actors or their environment. The production and consumption of cars, art, food, and much more include, of course, artistic, religious, moral, political, and many other aspects, but there are clearly also "economic" aspects to the production of art, or when a family harvests berries in the forest. The economy is made up of all these activities. Production can be coordinated in different ways, and what is produced can be distributed for consumption in different ways, which is to say that the market is one form of coordination among others. Nevertheless, the main point is that all of these coordination forms are inherently social. We will later return to the issue of "market economy," which consequently is a smaller part of what we call the economy. This will also bring up the central question of capitalism.

The Fundamental Economic Problem

Survival used to be the most direct problem that people faced and to some this is still the most pressing issue, as when an earthquake or flood throws a society into turmoil. However, by survival we generally mean the survival of the identities of economic actors.[3] A person who goes bankrupt is unlikely to die because of it – though at an early stage Durkheim (1992) recognized economic rupture as a cause of suicide. A firm which goes bankrupt ceases to exist, which is to say that this economic identity – the firm with its name – does not survive. Although few people's survival today depends exclusively on the market or even on economic wealth, we need only look at firms struggling to survive in periods of economic crisis to see that this is still the most fundamental problem.

In the process of cultivating the environment, people had to understand it, and through interpretations and "theories" of the world in which we live we have created order. The first interpretations were based on "religious" ideas, which could "explain" natural disasters, such as drought, lightning, or blizzards. Later, the natural sciences were developed as a tool to interpret the world, and more recently economic ideas have been used to interpret but also to change the economy.

It is in light of this general problem of survival, with the need to increase the quality of our predictions, that we must see other more concrete economic problems of order. The farmer, who in the spring sowed seed in the fields, assumed and hoped that enough could be harvested in the fall to feed the family. Seed was also required for the next year, perhaps with a need for increased returns, by giving it to someone in order to increase status, trading it for sheep, or – if an opportunity existed – by selling it in the market.

Farmers depend on the environment for their returns. Knowledge of the conditions, including the value of the output for the family and the processes of buying, selling, and, most likely, bargaining, is part of the experience and knowledge of being a farmer. Decision-making is facilitated when the environment – both the physical, in the form of, for example, the weather, and the social, in the form of, for example, laws and other institutions and market prices – is predictable.

Order increases predictability and is the opposite of chaos. *Order* refers to the predictability of human activities and the stability of social components in relation to each other. Actors in the economy try to control their environment (White 2008) and this is a way of generating order. The environment is largely made up of other economic actors, such as competitors, partners, buyers, and sellers. The degree of order can vary and attempts to control the environment can be made by single actors or in an organized fashion. Resources are a condition, but not enough, since actors cannot by definition control the responses from the environment that their attempts elicit. Human beings have, over time, controlled the environment with technologies, with – in the case of farming – tractors, fertilizers, and irrigation facilities, and also by organizing, including firms and even future markets, which enable farmers to sell what is produced before it has been harvested.

The need to create order with things and theories of things to survive is the key problem in the economy; this is often forgotten in economics. According to economics, the key problem in the economy is uncertainty (Keynes 1973; Knight 1921). *Uncertainty* refers to situations in which "we do not have a complete description of the world which we fully believe to be true" (Arrow 1974: 33–4). This means many states of the world are said to be true, but we do not know which one of them to choose. However, only when there is some order, or islands of order and some certainty, can we pose the question of *un*certainty. The question of uncertainty presupposes a given world and, in effect, presumes that the problem of order is solved. Thus, *ambiguity* refers to situations where it is unclear what there is, a condition that logically precedes uncertainty.

Today the economy is normally ordered, which turns the focus from ambiguity on to the problem of uncertainty; this, however, may shift quickly in times of financial havoc. It is thus uncertainty and, more concretely, uncertainty in relation to how production, consumption, and distribution are to be coordinated, which is the practical problem from the actors' perspective. For the individual consumer, this may be manifested in the question of how to fulfill their wants; for the businessman, it may be manifested in how to make a deal with a supplier; and for the politician, it may be manifested in further competition.

A first aspect of uncertainty refers to the uncertainty of the identity of economic actors, but also to the uncertainty concerning what culture and what *institutions* – informal and formal rules upheld over time by the sanctions imposed by a third party – are relevant in social life. A second aspect of uncertainty is that order facilitates calculation and the uncertainty discussed in economics is restricted to this aspect. Calculation is based on experience or on a priori calculations of known conditions, as Pareto argued. Risk implies that we can put a number on different means and ends, indicating that we can calculate the outcome. This is not possible in a situation of uncertainty, as Frank Knight (1921) made clear.[4] Uncertainty is, from this standpoint, to be avoided by actors, as it makes it difficult to predict and evaluate what can be done in the environment.

However, there is another side to uncertainty. Some uncertainty – or at least risk – is a driving force with regard to opportunities for profit in the economy; entrepreneurs cannot *know* the outcome of their actions (Schumpeter 2000). Thus, an entrepreneur, in contrast to a middleman, faces more profound uncertainty than whether he will profit from the structural arbitrage due to actors' position and access to knowledge in the social structure (Burt 1992). Given people's different knowledge and interests, and the limited knowledge each actor has of the economic system as a whole, there is always some uncertainty about the future. This may be reflected in the hope that the enterprise will enjoy a successful outcome, or any other motive of the actor. There are different ways of addressing the problems of order and uncertainty. We will next look at the ways in which economic actors can coordinate economic activities and resources for production, consumption, and distribution.

Forms of Coordination

The literature has identified three ideal-typical forms of social *coordination* – that is, bringing activities and things together to create order. Economic coordination through hierarchy (organization), networks, and markets (Granovetter 1985; Powell 1990; Thompson 2003) provides ways of solving the problems of production, consumption, and distribution. In reality, these structural forms hardly ever come in "pure" form, and we must separate them theoretically. This is not to deny, however, that one form dominates the others, and we may observe, for example, a market with strong elements of networks, or a network with some hierarchical structure.

In addition to network, hierarchy, and market, we will look at one additional form of coordination, which today is less common, namely autarchy, and yet others, such as heterarchy (Stark 2009), have been proposed. Autarchy – or self-government – together with the other forms will also serve as background for the discussion in chapter 3 of the historical making of markets. To outline the basic social formation in an ideal-typical way is the precondition for discussing how they are related in the real economy. The forms of coordination generate social order, but they do it in different ways, as each is characterized by its own type of social relations (cf. Polanyi 1957b). Polanyi, who essentially refers to economic coordination, speaks of reciprocity ("network"), redistribution ("hierarchy"), and markets. The fourth form that Polanyi describes, the autarchic household (*oikos*) can be regarded as an instance of hierarchy since it is "a trade-less hierarchical community directed to noneconomic ends, self-sufficiency (autarky) and the good life of the master" (Booth 1994: 212). Polanyi, moreover, does not believe that this form has had much relevance in history (Beckert 2007). We will look at these forms, first one by one, and then how they are combined and related to each other.

Network

No concept is more closely associated with new economic sociology than the network, although ideas vary widely regarding to what it refers. *Network* is here defined as several interwoven, dyadic (binary), ongoing interaction relations between actors (nodes), characterized by reciprocity. In contrast to the small group, in which all know each other, and the organized hierarchy of an organization, which is characterized by membership and central decision-making (Ahrne and Brunsson 2008), each actor in a network is at least connected to one other actor in the network, which makes it open and under no central control. Our definition of network is clearly different from the daily use of networks and, on the other, "network theory" as a form of research method. A network, moreover, is different from a sociogram,⁵ which can tie together "anything," regardless of the quality of the relationship. Furthermore, a network is by definition *not* organized, which is not to deny instrumentality in each or even all of its relations. We thus take a clear position that deviates from the idea that networks are forms of organization (Powell 1990). Networks can be described. Some actors (nodes) may be more central to a network, and "centrality" is a way of understanding the extent to which the network "revolves" around an actor.

Simmel introduced the phenomenology of networks into sociology. He developed an entire sociology based on what happens when one puts several dyads together, and how information and whatever else that "is" in the network can flow through some dyads but not others, and how this creates advantages and disadvantages for the actors as a result of their strategic and non-strategic actions (Simmel 1964). Furthermore, Simmel had already drawn the distinction between networks and markets, although not in these terms.

Network theory has been central in economic sociology (Swedberg 2003), thanks to its introduction by Harrison White and his students (Azarian 2003). White is the father of modern network theory and he has used it to analyze markets. However, he took the idea of networks from social anthropology. But others have made substantial contributions too, for example, Ronald Burt (1992), who has applied Simmel's ideas and coined the term "structural holes," which refers to missing social ties in the social structure. He has used the idea to analyze competition based on access to information. Entrepreneurs may, according to Burt, bridge the socio-spatial distance between actors and bind them together by filling holes in the social structure, thereby combining the different sets of information that different actors possess. Thus, entrepreneurs can profit from the combined effect of the knowledge and outperform rivals in the market. It is thus the structural position, rather than the unique personal traits, of actors that make them entrepreneurs.

Perhaps the best-known network study was by Mark Granovetter (1974), who looked at how people get jobs in the labor market. Neoclassical economics' explanation of why people get jobs is that people offer their labor in the market, which is characterized by more or less full information. In contrast, Granovetter finds that networks, which are not instrumentally established, are reciprocal information channels through which people find out about jobs. Granovetter found that information about new job openings was not freely available in the market, but came to people through their contacts. He also found that it was important to have many connections (ties) to others, and particularly to people with whom the actors have less in common. These "weak" ties provide information that the actor is less likely to get from "strong" ties (for example, ties with whom they have frequent interaction).[6] This study shows how information travels back and forth in networks. The network is then a resource of coordinating activities for all the actors who are part of it.

In contemporary society, "to network," used as a verb, has become common, and some people may tell us that they are members of a network. But as soon as there is control and a membership, and people or firms "join" a "network" to gain information, we are getting closer to organization and organized coordination, which means that at least two actors come together and decide on the order of the market (cf. Ahrne and Brunsson 2008). There is, in other words, no "free rider" problem in "pure" networks; this problem can emerge only in relation to organized coordination.

It is clear that network theory in new economic sociology represents a structural perspective (Swedberg 2003: 37–40). The initial idea of networks – which we follow here – has its origins in studies conducted by anthropologists. Malinowski's study of the so-called Kula-ring is a classical example of how trade is *embedded*, a notion which here refers to the structural relations which enable or hinder activities in a large cultural framework, as well as in specific concrete network relations (Granovetter 1985). But this form of trade cannot be understood unless we bring in culture. The critique that sociologists such as Viviana Zelizer have directed toward structural economic sociology – which, in practice, is often identical with network theory – is that it excludes culture. This critique should be taken seriously. By turning to social anthropology, we can see how the network is a central coordination form in the economy. How may we explain the "economic sociology" (Malinowski 1922: 167) of the Kula trading system that Malinowski studied in the archipelagoes of Melanesian New Guinea?

Malinowski lived in this area from 1914 to 1918 and had the opportunity to conduct an indepth field study. His aim was to understand the islanders' activities in their own terms, instead of applying a modernistic toolkit, such as neoclassical theory. His empirical field was made up of several islands, populated by different tribes. Although the tribes differ, he says that in some "[t]here is no institution of regular chieftainship, nor have they any system of rank or caste" (Malinowski 1922: 41). That order was not maintained through the means of hierarchy does not imply chaos; the oldest people have most influence in a matrilineal ordered society (Malinowski 1922: 37), which means social positions, as well as wealth, are inherited in the maternal line. This must be said in contrast to "the existence of rank and social differentiation" (Malinowski 1922: 52), as well as the clear chieftainship that he observed on the Trobriand Islands, his main object of study.

Malinowski's study shows how the social, economic, aesthetic, cultural, and magical lives of the islanders were interwoven in such a way that one cannot truly separate them; it is only by an analytic act of interpretation or even translation (Quine 1964), based on modern conceptions, that this "construction" is generated. More generally, and of great interest to us, is his account of "the economy," which cannot be separated from the history and description of the tribes' language and biological and social relations. Magic plays a central role, and activities in which the people in the archipelago are involved, such as journeys with canoes or a "fierce and daring cannibal and head hunting expedition" (Malinowski 1922: 39), are subject to rituals and magical "interpretations." The magical rites and spells are certainly not merely passive activities for interpretation or "performed" to rationalize actions already taken; they are active and constitutive of the world, as they affect the outcomes of what people undertake.

The overarching institution which Malinowski identifies for understanding the activities in his field – including those that are "economic" – is the Kula ring, or the Kula exchange. This exchange is based on the dyadic Kula relationship. When all of the Kula relationships are taken together, we have a representation of the network of relations that bind people together. The Kula exchange refers to the exchange of ceremonial gifts (Malinowski 1922: 95). A person gives something to a partner with whom he is in a Kula relationship, and later, as this is a male activity, he gets something in return. But in contrast to barter or money exchange, the "counter-gift is left to the giver, and it cannot be enforced by any kind of coercion" (Malinowski 1922: 96). However, this is not at all a situation that boils down to calculations, as suggested in game theory. It is based on reciprocity rooted in culture and what is "taken for granted"; this is what one does if one is in the Kula-ring. These "exchanges" are regulated by rules and conventions – in other words, by culture – so that the "Kula is not a surreptitious and precarious form of exchange. It is, quite the contrary, rooted in myth, backed by traditional law, and surrounded with magical rites" (Malinowski 1922: 85).

If we look at the islands as positioned in relation to each other as a circle, the trade circuits many – though not all – of them. The exchanges are structured so that the islands that make up the "circle" are tied to each other in such a way that one exchanges most frequently with neighboring islands, and thus only indirectly with people who are located far away, who are more difficult to reach with canoes. What is exchanged? In one direction of the ring, long necklaces of red shells and, in the other direction, bracelets of white shells. The point of the exchange of shells is to receive them, hold on to them for some time, and finally to pass them on to members of another tribe with whom one has a tie. The central aspect is that "'once in the Kula, always in the Kula', and a partnership between two men is a permanent and lifelong affair" (Malinowski 1922: 83), which is to say that the Kula ring constitutes the social being of those involved and, indirectly, those excluded from the ring. However, a person has not only one "Kula-partner"; it is the multitude – but still limited number – of dyads that make it an institution in the form of a network. The Kula system has evolved over a long period, and Malinowski says that those who take part "have no knowledge of the *total outline*" of this "social construction" (Malinowski 1922: 83).

Malinowski is clear about the centrality of the Kula network: "Nor can this wide network of social co-relations and cultural influences be considered for a moment as ephemeral, new or precarious" (Malinowski 1922: 510). The exchange of shells is connected to the trade of other items. In fact, Malinowski identifies seven different forms of exchange, but six of them are forms of gift-giving and only one is "trade, pure and simple" (Malinowski 1922: 177–91). There is, however, no market, though ongoing processes of gift exchange may turn into market exchange.

We have now discussed the notion of network at some length, and shown how this relationship is characterized by reciprocity. This idea was also applied extensively to the empirical case that Malinowski provided, and one reason for taking this old example of a network is to show how it builds as well as represents trust among "savages," to whom cannibalism was, at least when Malinowski was around, an alternative. The network is the foremost form of economic coordination between people of different tribes. Thus, "all around the ring of Kula there is a network of relationships, and . . . naturally the whole forms one interwoven fabric" (Malinowski 1922: 92), and this is a way of trying to control the environment, composed of other humans and nature.

As an added value, we can see how these "economic" actions were "embedded" in a web of social relations, which is also the central theme of Marcel Mauss's book *The Gift* (Mauss 2002). Gifts are reciprocal and a way of creating a tie. The network is the structural form made up of ties in which "cultural," "political," and "economic" interactions are interwoven as much as they are constituted. In other words, the tribe becomes what it is in relation to other tribes as result of the interaction. We must, thus, more generally see how the Kula exchange is part of, as well as facilitating, trade, as it enables credit and generates trust between those who are involved in the exchange (Malinowski 1922: 86). We will return to the central idea of networks, not least in a discussion of how markets are related.

Hierarchy

In organizational sociology, which is another important source of inspiration for economic sociologists (Swedberg 2003), hierarchy is the most commonly discussed form of coordination, as almost all firms are variations of hierarchies. Hierarchy is, in contrast to networks, an order based on decision (Ahrne and Brunsson 2008: 51) in which resources are concentrated and governed from a center. *Hierarchy* is defined as actors in positions at different ranks, organized in one administrative body so that orders can be given and actions performed. Relations in hierarchies are asymmetric, as, for example, between the two roles of superior and subordinate in an organization. The connection between organization and hierarchy is strong, and the notion seems occasionally to refer to organization. It is clear that "formal organizations were patterned on early bureaucracies" (White 2008: 210), and the origin of bureaucracy is the military hierarchy. Hierarchy is essential in an organization, but an organization is of course characterized by additional elements, such as culture, rules, membership, and resources.

Taylorism is the application of scientific principles to economic production in an organized form. In practice, it is a way of coordinating people, capital, and machines in accordance with bureaucratic principles within an organization. This means that superiors decide what subordinates should do. The task of every person is essentially determined by their position in the hierarchy. This means that one can talk of a hierarchy with roles, each of which is associated with clear rules and expectations concerning what to do. Let us look more closely at the coordination of garment production as an example.

The production – and let us here restrict ourselves to the sewing – of shirts has remained essentially the same since sewing machines were introduced in the production of garments in the first half of the nineteenth century. This was one technical innovation that made industrial production easier. To sell fabrics and clothes to the masses, industrial production was rationalized and organized according to hierarchical principles in the form of bureaucracy.

Max Weber (whose last name means "weaver" in German) was born into a family who owned a textile plant. Weber himself conducted studies of workers in this factory, providing him with first-hand knowledge of the reality of workers' lives and how work was organized. He informs us that discipline in organizations applying scientific management can be traced to its military heritage (Weber 1978: 1156–7). Scientific management is a form of economic bureaucracy. Following Parsons's interpretation, the main characteristics of bureaucracy are: "rationality, resting on a complex, hierarchically organized division of tasks, each with a sharply marked off sphere of 'competence'; specialization of functions, whereby a special premium is placed upon expert knowledge . . . and impersonality" (1929: 37).

Calculability merits particular attention in this context. The form of (economic) bureaucracy that Weber studies, a hierarchy that operates according to the general intentions of its owners, is well adapted to an economy and markets characterized by relative stability. Weber connects bureaucracy and, in particular, the calculability of the Taylorist system – which is also called "scientific management" – with its principles for organizing labor and work (Weber 1978: 101–3, 150, 974–5).

In hierarchies, in contrast to the transfer of gifts in networks and the exchange of one thing for another in markets, property rights do not change hands. Everything that is "traded" between members of the organization still belongs to the organization or, in the case of a firm, to the owners of the firm.

In practice, bureaucracy is often related to both hierarchies and markets. Furthermore, bureaucratic organizations attract their staff in the labor market. And, by employing people in the labor markets, firms get workers who obey the rules of the organization. They are, as it were, under a contract. Still, a worker may end such a contract and thereby reappear on the labor market. In contrast to goods, which have no will of their own, a worker is both an offer and a seller who owns this property.

Combining Forms of Coordination

It is now possible to summarize the discussion of forms of coordination. Given the economic problem of coordinating production (or consumption), it is possible to present the different forms graphically, as in figure 2.1. The market, to repeat, has buyers and sellers. Its characteristic traits are evaluation, choice, and competition. The network is characterized by reciprocity, or "give and take," but no competition. Finally, hierarchy is characterized by centralized power and giving orders, but no transfer of property rights. All forms are capable of producing output, given a certain input, but they do it in different ways.

These three forms are important for the coordination of consumption. In many traditional societies, as described by Malinowski, Mauss, and others, resources are distributed and eventually consumed according to reciprocal relations. In a hierarchy, such as a prison, each inmate is given a portion of food decided, directly or indirectly, by the prison governor. Consumption coordinated in the market means that people are allowed to consume (or save) only what they have obtained in the market(s). In most cases, the state imposes restrictions on people in the market by collecting taxes. These taxes can then be used for redistribution, and

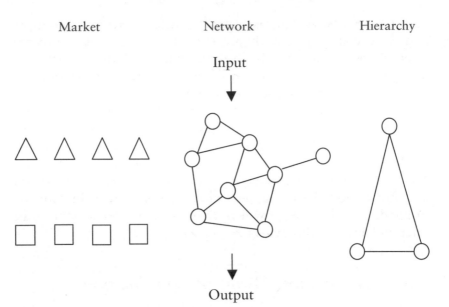

Figure 2.1 Coordination of production based on input, market, network, and hierarchy. The market is characterized by buyers and sellers. In reality, these three ideal-types are found in mixed forms.

thus change the outcomes of market transactions, according to the state, or the actors who control the state (Korpi 1983).

The different forms of coordination – network, hierarchy, and market – are ways of reducing complexity and, above all, of creating order in the environment, to enable production, distribution, and consumption. This is not to say that uncertainty is the key question for the actors themselves, nor to present a functional argument. The coordination forms are presented here as ideal-types, but there are of course variations in real life, so that we also encounter everyday notions such as "organized network" (Thompson 2003: 28–9) and hybrid forms (Williamson 1991). In other words, economists also accept that markets may intersect with hierarchies (Bowles and Gintis 2000: 1422).

The different forms of coordination make up one another's environment. The environment of an actor in a firm is largely made up of others in the same economic organization, in the form of a hierarchy. The environment of a firm is mainly made up of other firms in a market, and the environment of a market, in a similar fashion, is other markets. Some people in the same hierarchy exchange information in the form of a market, and firms may collaborate in a network to maintain a certain price level. Furthermore, a market is related to other markets, and the firms in the same market may join hands in a meta organization (Ahrne and Brunsson 2008), for example, to protect their collective interests. The state, organized as a hierarchy, may monitor markets as well as firms.

Firms – to take the example of one kind of economic actor that is organized as a hierarchy – try to impose order within their own ranks, by controlling their staff. This process is complicated by the problem of the conflict of interest between the owner of the firm and the CEO(s) who run the business on a daily basis – the so-called principal–agent problem. Control projects proposed by different interests within the firm may lead to struggles over the internal determination of control (Fligstein 2001: 69). But it is important to recognize that firms may also try to construct and thereby control their environment (Ahrne 1994: 104). One way to do this, as Fligstein (2001) says, is to control the market in which they mainly obtain their identity.

Examples of how coordination forms are intertwined in real economic life are not hard to find, and looking more closely at this will also take us to the discussion of how, when, and why specific forms are used. Also, at the personal and intimate level, we can observe the blending of forms of coordination. Zelizer has shown how social relations of reciprocity, best described as networks, are mixed with economic transactions that are more characteristic of markets. She sees that caring for family members shows "contestable mixes of caring and economic transactions" (2005c: 162). This suggests that in-house care also exhibits an "incessant buzz of economic production, consumption, distribution, and transfers of assets within households" (2005c: 172), which one may perhaps expect only from professional care purchased in markets. Trade fairs are an arena in which social relations are built, but they are also market places. The geographers Power and Jansson (2008) describe how trade shows, taking place in different cities throughout the year, serve both as a market place for comparing alternatives, including a labor market, and as an arena for establishing relations and cooperation. Trade fairs are good examples of how markets and networks are not separate, but often combined (Skov 2006). Related to this is the importance of gift-giving, in which sales personnel, who try to build up market relations, are involved (Darr 2006). These relations are not reducible to attempts to tie social bonds to make more profit, as social bonds are often a condition of doing business.

However, friendship and other forms of reciprocal relations in markets can be turned into a facade of competition, as when firms use strategies "to cooperate with competitors in order to share markets. Cartels, publicized prices, barriers to entry, limited production, patents, licensing agreements, and joint ventures in marketing and production are all tactics that firms use to divide markets" (Fligstein 2001: 71). One must thus always remember that it is the "third party," as suggested by Simmel (1964, 1983), who benefits from competition in the market, not necessarily the sellers as a group.

Arthur Stinchcombe has analyzed why firms use the market to find partners in large construction projects. Stinchcombe (1992) developed the idea of craft-organized production. His key idea is that the uncertainty and flux which are characteristic of projects in the construction industry lead to non-bureaucratic organizations (cf. Zuckerman 1999). Subcontractors may come together to work on unique projects. This means that the firm hires the special "knowledge" of different organizations needed for each unique production rather than organizing itself as a large hierarchy. This idea was later used by Paul Hirsch (1992) in a study of the production of cultural goods. Examples of cultural goods are "movies, plays, books, art prints, phonograph records, and pro football games; each is nonmaterial in the sense that it embodies a live, one-of-a-kind performance and/or contains a unique set of ideas" (Hirsch 1992: 365). Hirsch argues that the uncertainty in cultural sectors whose products are characterized by changing fads and fashion is organized in terms of projects. This means that, for each task, a team of experts is put together for that particular job. The tasks, emerging out of the market, are so different and so unique that no one organization is capable of having sufficient internal resources to cover all eventualities. In other words, actors may overcome the uncertainty of the market by not relying on a purely hierarchical organization. The market, however, is not the sole form of coordination in cultural production. It is in the interest of advertising agencies to build relationships with their clients, thereby reducing uncertainty by blocking the market and its competition. The clients, in contrast, wish to disengage, precisely to maintain the possibility of evaluating and comparing different advertising agencies, using the market as a benchmark (Baker, Faulkner, and Fisher 1998).

Perhaps the most common finding in the new economic sociology with regard to markets is that we identify aspects, stronger or weaker, of network coordination in markets. Long-lasting relations which last for decades between buyers and sellers in markets are not uncommon (Macaulay 1963: 63). Wayne Baker (1990) has shown how the relationship between firms and their banks is a "hybrid" of long-term (network) and short-term (market) relations. In another study, Brian Uzzi (1997) shows how firms collaborate across the market. In Uzzi's study it is not hierarchy that is the focus, but markets and networks. Based on ethnographic research in the New York garment industry among women's better-quality dress firms, Uzzi shows that the uncertainty firms face can be diminished by not keeping market relations at arm's length. Uzzi argues that firms can control at least some elements of uncertainty by building bridges across the market. We must underline that this does not primarily change the organizational form within firms. The focus is on the relationship between firms. The network relations, which may persist for years, facilitate exchanges of ideas and allow both sides to "give and take" in a way that is balanced over time. The trust-based relationship enables firms to move faster, as they do not have to negotiate with each other. It also facilitates the transfer of information and enables firms to jointly solve problems. This effect of speed is of crucial importance in the fashion industry, which is characterized by rapid changes. Uzzi's study analyzes a situation in which spatial distances are limited and physical proximity is part of what explains why there can be a trust relationship. Aspers (2010) has demonstrated in a study of the garment industry that this type of relationship may stretch around the globe. He also finds business relations which may have existed for years are "benchmarked" against the market, which is a way in which firms can avoid becoming over-embedded (Uzzi 1997: 58). Baker and Faulkner (1993) have shown how market actors in the heavy electrical equipment industry were tied to each other in such a way that they could control prices. More generally, we must not forget what everyone operating in an industry knows, namely, that contacts play a key role in obtaining information. In this sense there is no industry in which actions are coordinated through markets alone. This body of research comprises merely some examples of studies that show the reality of many, though not all, industries, namely that economic actors in markets are often embedded in social networks (Granovetter 1985).

Markets and other forms of coordination presuppose the trust characteristic of networks. The trust needed to engage in the market is institutionally rooted and an essential part of the world in which the person grows up. Following this line of argumentation, it makes no sense to see trust as an outcome of rational calculations. This is to say that contracts are not only embedded in trust (Bowles and Gintis 2000: 1424), but can only be made given the existence of basic trust (Durkheim 1984; Möllering 2006). We may tentatively conclude that competition in markets makes it possible to relate what is done within a firm (hierarchy) (cf. Coase 1937, 1988; Williamson 1981), as well as in the network (cf. Burt 1992), to the alternative that the market offers.

Markets Embedded in Markets

We have so far seen that markets coexist with other forms of coordination and that they are interrelated. This is an important insight, but it should not be the focus of a book on markets. We must not forget that markets are often – and in some cases mainly – related to other markets. One may, following Harrison White (2002b), say that markets are embedded in markets. What is involved in a market being embedded in another market? Let us take the simple example of the garments we purchase in a store. The consumer market is made up of firms with stable identities which have positions as sellers in relation to each other, but each of these firms, when they "turn around," operate as buyers (Aspers 2010). When they buy fabrics, hire labor, or use the services of banks they operate as buyers in these markets. Sellers in these markets, for example, workers, are themselves buyers in yet other markets, such as food, housing, and banks. In this case, we may say that the markets are located in a production chain, so that we can talk of markets in "upstream" and "downstream" relations, as seen from a certain market (White 2002b). This form of relationship has been demonstrated in several industries, such as the garment industry and the car industry (Gereffi, Humphrey, and Sturgeon 2005). In these industries, there is often one leading market, from which other markets and their actors are governed. An *industry*, as we define this notion today, is a set of markets, one of which is the core or leading market, and to which other markets are auxiliary. In the fashion industry, the final consumer markets are the core markets, and the labor, service (including advertisement), and commodity markets that, substantially, are oriented to the selling of garments, are part of this industry. It is often suppliers who operate in markets upstream of the production chain who are forced to adapt to the terms set by the firms in the leading market. What actors in one market can do depends on what actors in other markets do. In short, the markets are embedded in each other or, as we have also put it: the environment of a market is to a large extent other markets.

An important aspect of markets that are embedded in each other is that they enable economic coordination across markets. An actor who has an idea about something she might like to sell may be able to calculate the price of what she will offer, even though there is no market for this product yet. The condition is that there are markets for the input materials and services needed to calculate the cost side (Hayek 1945).

Buying and selling systems between departments within an organization is one example of internal markets, which are encircled by an organization. A special case of these quasi-markets – or "markets within markets" – has been created in large industries, such as the car industry. Different plants owned by the same firm, often located in different countries, have been forced to enter into internal competition. In this case, we should speak of internal markets. The competition in this case may end with more orders or resources going to the plants which outperform the others. More often, however, the competition results in the closure of the plants that come out worst in the evaluation process. The reason for closure may not be the efficiency of the workers, but also institutional factors, such as tax levels, exchange rates, and other aspects that are outside of the control of the plant.

Internal labor markets are another example of markets that are embedded within a hierarchy, and this hierarchy is itself embedded in the market of the firm. In this case, competition is restricted to those already inside the organization. They may, moreover, not compete on price, as wages are usually fixed, but on their qualifications or personality or whatever is being judged to obtain the position which is "open." This competition inside an organization creates so-called vacancy chains, in which the jobs left by high-ranking members of the organization are filled by someone from a lower position, who in turn leaves a position that has to be filled. The larger the organization is, and the further up in the hierarchy a position must be filled, the more extensive the chain reaction (White 1970).

Another version of not incomplete markets are so-called "quasi-markets" which have emerged when, for example, welfare states have tried to increase the output of health care, schools, and other services. These "quasi-markets" are "set up in such a way that the provision of services remains free at the point of delivery: no money changes hands between the final users (for example, pupils, patients) and the provider of the services (for example, schools, hospitals)" (Popper, Bartlett, and Wilson 1994: 1–2). Although these "markets" may appear to meet the short definition provided above, there are two problems. The rights are not fully owned by the users, and these markets fail to meet the third prerequisite of markets, namely, that the value of the product must be established in the market (as this is done politically or, potentially, in another market). The property rights are divided among several hands and not exchanged in the market. Furthermore, the roles of "buyers" and "sellers" are not clear, and nor are the interests of the three parties involved: users, producers, and the state that pays for the product or service. Quasi-markets, although not markets strictly speaking, may nonetheless be seen as part of the general trend of marketization.

Relations of Economic Coordination

How is it possible to explain the coordination form actually in use and what form ought to be used? In chapter 3, we will discuss both the historical reasons for the emergence of what has been called "market society" (Slater and Tonkiss 2001) and the various ethical positions with regard to markets and market society. Here we concentrate on two demands which apply to all economic coordination.

The forms of coordination and the ways they are used must be legitimate and economically viable. Legitimacy is not restricted to markets, but to all kinds of coordination, economic or otherwise. It implies that the form used is legal and/or morally acceptable in the specific environment in which it is used. Networks may not be accepted as the central coordination form in a competition for constructing a municipal school; in fact, this would most likely be called a trust, which undermines the idea of market competition. Controlling the environment enables firms in a market to increase their legitimacy, but firms that bribe politicians or civil servants are also trying to control their environment, though in an illegitimate way.

The first condition of any form of coordination is that it is legitimate among those taking part, as well as in its environment. This means that it has to be culturally acceptable. It is unlikely that a pure market exchange could have occurred among those taking part in the network-oriented Kula-ring exchange described by Malinowski. The existence of anti-trust laws shows that coordination by networks or hierarchies is forbidden in some settings; only market coordination is legitimate. Normally, for a firm that obeys the law and behaves in the manner expected of a market participant, legitimacy is not the main problem.

However, a coordination form must be not only legitimate, but also economically viable, and for most economic actors this is a larger problem. This refers to the problem of survival in an environment. The survival of an individual economic actor, whether a person, an organization, or a collective of actors, is conditioned by the environment. Furthermore, economic viability is second in rank after legitimacy. The cultural and ethical condition that legitimizes forms is of superior rank. It is only within the accepted framework of coordination forms that one can choose and make an "economic," "efficient," "solidaristic," or "democratic" evaluation to ascertain the "best" form of coordination (Boltanski and Thévenot 2006).

The Market as the Benchmark of Efficiency

Given that all forms of coordination are legitimate, we have to determine which is the most equitable or the most efficient. How can we judge their efficiency? One way is to benchmark them. Benchmarking means evaluating them according to an established standard. There is, of course, no "established standard" as the point is to compare them. The market plays a special role as it is characterized by the evaluation of various alternatives. However, we can also compare different qualities, given a price, or different prices for a certain quality, or – although this is more complex – a number of different variables at a time (Chamberlin 1948, 1953). The market is, in this way, reflexive, as the market can be used to evaluate not only other coordination forms, but also other markets.

What role does this benchmarking capacity play for those taking part in markets? The market is the form of coordination that enables actors who occupy roles as buyers and sellers to switch relations and compete in an arena that evaluates actors or their offers. This evaluation implies "a measure of shelter from the uncertainties of the business" (White 2002b: 1). But how can it be a shelter? No form of coordination is a shelter, but the market is the only form that is characterized by evaluation. This means that it can serve as a benchmark of efficiency.

It is only in this light – that of the economic actor who has to determine how to act in a situation of limited information – that we can see the special role markets have in relation to other forms of coordination. It is only in the market that evaluations are based on the principle of comparison of offers, a benchmark which can lead to competition and selection (Simmel 1923; Weber 1978: 38–40). Furthermore, it is only in relation to the benchmark of the market and, more specifically, market prices, that the "efficiency" of hierarchies (firms) and networks can be evaluated, which suggests that markets play a special role in the economy. Thus, competition in markets makes it possible to relate what is done within a firm (hierarchy) (cf. Coase 1937, 1988; Williamson 1981), as well as in networks (cf. Burt 1992), to the alternative that the market offers. The social relations in markets are, ideal-typically, found at so-called "arm's length," which is another way of describing the kind of competition that involves deals with a determinate end, which is assumed in neoclassical textbooks (cf. Uzzi 1997). This brief discussion suggests that many problems affecting organizations and networks can be addressed only in relation to how they are embedded in markets, and its evaluation process.

But why do we need this benchmarking? Why cannot we simply plan the economy, given the enormous amount of information that is available? This is the socialist dream, but all attempts so far have ended in failure. Hayek has an explanation of why central planning does not result in efficiency: "the 'data' from which the economic calculus starts are never for the whole society 'given' to a single mind which could work out the implications, and can never be so given" (Hayek 1945: 519). Thus, the problem is much more a problem of information processing and interpretation – that is, a knowledge problem – than a problem of information. This "knowledge problem" is solved – and, Hayek says, in the best way – by the signaling effects of prices in markets (Spence 2002). This means that knowledge is distributed among people, but there is no omnipotent actor, or organization, that can know people's ends or the best means to achieve them. To Hayek, society's coordination problem, instead, is to "secure the best use of resources known to any of the members of society, for ends whose relative importance only these individuals know" (Hayek 1945: 520). Hayek's argument is that "in a system where the knowledge of the relevant facts is dispersed among many people, prices can act to coordinate the separate actions" (Hayek 1945: 526). In this way, Hayek argues, prices communicate information in a way that enables the evaluation of the alternative uses of the resources available to each individual actor.

We must make it clear that this evaluation is restricted to one of the ends that economic actions, and actors, must take into account, namely, efficiency or "rational economic organization" (Calıskan and Callon 2009; Hayek 1945: 520) and, more generally, the survival of the enterprises or economic actors. This is not, however, the benchmark of legitimacy. The market is arguably a superior form of evaluating coordination forms for efficiency, but it does not follow that it can adjudicate in matters of morals, aesthetics, politics, and religion. When we want to evaluate what is most democratic, the market may not be the benchmark to use. We have, for example, noted that the "benchmarking" required for a market to exist is, in the first place, an ethical decision; only when a market is seen as acceptable in a given setting can it come into existence. Discussion of the assumptions central to understanding how different social scientists can come to radically different viewpoints concerning the usefulness of markets will continue in chapter 3.

Summary

This chapter has focused on ways in which economic actors have to cope with the problem of economic survival. To control the environment, create order, and in cases of order to overcome uncertainty, actors may establish social relations while pursuing economic activities. There are, as we have seen, different ways of coordinating economic activities. We have looked at networks, hierarchies, and markets from an analytic perspective. All these social forms are structural ways of creating order and coordinating production, consumption, and distribution. It is only in relation to other forms of coordination that it is possible to make sense of markets, which also explains why we have included these other forms in the book. When we discussed Malinowski's study, it became clear that the structural form of network can be understood only in relation to content, hence values and culture are essential components, as "relations" never exist "as such," that is, as "empty pipelines" in which content "flows." We made this separation for analytic purposes, and in the next chapter we begin to unfold the motivational and cultural values involved in economic activities.

Although this chapter did not focus on markets, they were highlighted for the possibility of evaluation they offer. The capacity for evaluation, competition, and rivalry provides markets with a certain benchmarking function. Only with the help of "markets" can forms of coordination, including markets, be evaluated from the perspective of efficiency. In the next chapter, we will see that this "economic" autonomy – which means that coordination is evaluated on the basis of economic values – is far from the only possibility. In history, "religious" values have dominated, while moral and political values are also used in the discussion of what offers are allowed to be traded in markets, how wealth is to be distributed, and how markets are controlled. This will also take us to the discussion of the ethical aspects of markets.

3

Markets in Social Life

Markets are probably the least researched form of coordination – and, at the same time, perhaps the most enigmatic. This may appear strange, but there is one clear explanation of why this is the case in economics that was mentioned in the first chapter: since markets are "natural," and therefore a starting point, they are often used to explain other phenomena rather than considered as objects in need of explanation. From a sociological standpoint, markets are indeed in need of explanation, however, especially as they come in many forms. Looking at their role in history and tracing their historical emergence is an important task.

The economic view on markets has become central in political and public debate. This is merely a reflection of the fact that the market is the form of social organization that is growing at the expense of the other two forms (hierarchies and networks). There are several reasons for this, including the demise of communism (e.g., Nee and Matthews 1996; Nee and Opper 2006) and corresponding political decisions to introduce a market economy into such large countries as Russia and China. Markets are seen as the solution to particular political problems, with a corresponding attempt to make these countries attractive to foreign investors (Bandelj 2009b). They also have a central role in development research (Kiely 2007), as well as in the demand for shareholder value (cf. Zuckerman 2000). Markets, however, are not newly developed social formations, and to account historically for their diffusion is a central task of this chapter.

To understand the history of markets is crucial to reaching an understanding of our own time. This question takes us to a related question: why is it that the market has expanded, over several hundred years, at the expense of hierarchy and network? We claim that the analytic distinctions between the important forms of coordination – network, hierarchy, and market – must be seen in relation to historical processes of the gradual differentiation of societal spheres. Special attention is therefore devoted to the emergence of the economic sphere as relatively autonomous from other spheres of life, most notably the religious sphere. This will also take us to the issue of capitalism and market ideology, and eventually to the assumptions of man, on which market theories rest. This chapter, in other words, looks more closely at the cultural underpinning of markets. We will see that markets must be legitimate. It will also be shown that there can be different motivational forces within markets.

Interpreting Markets in History

The issue of markets in history has been approached from a number of different perspectives and disciplines. One is history – or, more specifically, economic history – another is archaeology, and a third, anthropology. Although these perspectives are necessary, and indeed represent a major contribution to the sociological understanding of markets, two things must be said about their status. The first is that the empirical material, as always, is loaded with theory. In the case of the history of markets, it is the neoclassical mainstream and, in some cases, Marxist economic ideas that have guided the research and thus shaped interpretation.

The second problem with historical studies is more profound: the lack of data. In particular, archaeological research – and here we are referring to prehistoric conditions, before the written word – is difficult to use for the purposes of sociological research. Within this tradition the problems are so great that there is even discussion of "methodological optimism" as a way out of the predicament (Earl 2000: 48). We argue that it is not very fruitful to try to put together a picture of the market from the pieces offered by archaeology. In trying to understand how markets were made, we will draw mainly on two bodies of research: work by historians based on historical documents, and work by anthropologists based on studies of societies with no, or limited, contact with modern Western cultures. However, we will use a sociological approach to interpret this material. More generally, using contemporary ways of thinking, concepts, and theories in order to try to understand the past is a necessity from which we cannot escape; it is the condition of all attempts at understanding, as hermeneutics has shown (Gadamer 1990; Heidegger 2001b).[1]

Market Making in History

Study of the roots of modern markets reveals that markets are interlinked with and shaped within the society and culture of a particular period. The historical perspective presented here shows how markets are made and serves as a general background to the discussion of modern markets, but also as evidence in the discussion of how markets have evolved (cf. chapter 7).

In this section, we set out to discuss these different forms of economic "exchange." We differentiate analytically between the dominant forms of economic exchange: (a) sharing in the community; (b) the exchange of gifts; (c) barter; (d) dyadic trade; and (e) fairs and market exchange (figure 3.1).

We argue that exchange in the form of fairs and markets grew in parallel with the complexity of a society affected by population growth, functional differentiation, and cultural and technological development, which can be summarized as rationalization. It is important to note that we use the concept of social and cultural embeddedness to explain the process of differentiation whereby distribution in the community was succeeded by more complex forms of exchange, such as fairs and markets.

Research on markets can be summarized by two points: first, economic transactions and commerce are not restricted to markets; in fact, a wide variety of forms has been observed. The

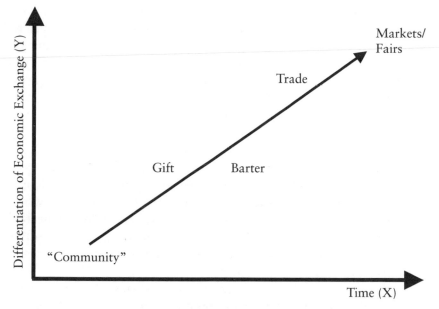

Figure 3.1   Forms of economic exchange

Note: This figure illustrates the analytically differentiated dominant forms of exchange (Y) which evolved historically (X). The differentiation is a non-teleological process and the formerly dominant forms of coordination persist and thus exist in parallel with markets.

notion of market, as we have mentioned, refers both to the price mechanism and the place where trade is conducted, but it is clear that the market mechanism, as described by economists, is not the starting point in the history of commerce (Braudel 1992). Second, reciprocity in communities, the household economy, and redistribution in hierarchical organization are economic forms of transaction, which only later were supplemented by market exchange (Polanyi 1957a).

It is useful first to clarify the origin of the notion of "market." Market as a phenomenon is older than the term. The word is of Latin origin (*mercatus*, trade), possibly with an Etruscan root, and related to more general aspects of the economy. This suggests that the term could be almost 3,000 years old. The Roman god of trade and the bringer of messages was called Mercurius, and we know that the Roman mythology reflects the Greek mythology. The Greek equivalent god – Hermes – was the god not only of travelers and commerce in general, but also of thieves. Seen in the light of etymology, Romans both upgraded and civilized commerce when they took over the Greek mythology. The door-to-door selling ("peddling," *Hausiervertrieb* in German) that the Romans – at least at the time of Julius Caesar – practiced was called *Markt* by the Germans (Grimm and Grimm 1971: 12, Sp 1644–53). In those days the traveling tradesmen were traveling "strangers," who may not have been trusted by everyone, but who in addition to their goods also – like Hermes and Mercurius – were bringing news to the people who themselves were firmly rooted. The word is thus traceable to roaming trade, and was only later connected to a place. Only when traveling traders frequented an area so the buyers could form ideas of price and quality relations, can we speak of some early form of competition.

The similarity of the equivalent terms in various European languages – *mercado* in Spanish, *marché* in French, and *marknad* in Norwegian, to take a few examples – suggests that the concept was diffused together with the practice. Hence, though the phenomenology of the market, of which competition is an essential component, is very old, the term "market," from what we know, only gradually acquired this meaning. Originally, it referred to what we today call "trade." Let us now turn to the different economic relations which will inform us about the origin of the market, but which also help us to demarcate markets from other forms of commerce in the widest sense.

Gift and exchange

The starting point of all forms of trade may well have been gifts between tribes which were exchanged in complex social networks of people, such as the already mentioned Kula-trading circuit (cf. chapter 2). Malinowski's study teaches us that archaic trading circuits were highly "organized" and ritualized by the rules of the trading process that formed the basis for stable social relations in and between tribes. The other crucial point we can take from

Malinowski's study is that tribal economies cannot be described as a form of "natural economy," free of power structures and social stratification, populated with economic men. Consequently, he rejects the universality of motivational forces for economic action, as assumed in neoclassical theory: "Gain, such as is often the stimulus for work in more civilized communities, never acts as an impulse to work under the original native conditions" (Malinowski 1922: 156). The basis of almost every social interaction in these tribes was a constant and obligatory reciprocal giving and taking. Although the Trobrianders practiced instrumental forms of the exchange of goods by bartering and haggling, this form of trade was seen as inferior to others because it lacked the magical and mystical grounding in the very purpose of society itself (Malinowski 1922: 166–91).

Marcel Mauss (2002), a nephew and student of Émile Durkheim, referred to the studies of contemporary anthropologists to formulate a general theory of symbolic exchange. An example from the Maori can clarify this theory (Mauss 2002: 10–13): In the Maori language, every gift is possessed by the "hau." The hau is spiritual power which is part of the giver's soul. Mauss describes it as an informal form of obligation which reminds the receiver to reciprocate with an equally valued counter gift: "What imposes obligation in the present received and exchanged, is the fact that the thing received is not inactive. Even when it has been abandoned by the giver, it still possesses something of him" (Mauss 2002: 15).

The social constraints and the informal obligations of exchange, such as the norm of reciprocation, can even lead to the destruction of valuable items, as in the "War of Property" (Mauss 2002: 47) in the potlatch practiced by tribes in northern Alaska. The most extravagant form of potlatch is when the chief destroys his own goods to demonstrate his superiority: "Whole boxes of olachen (candlefish) oil or whale oil are burnt, as are houses and thousands of blankets. The most valuable copper objects are broken and thrown into the water, in order to crush and to 'flatten' one's rival. In this way one not only promotes oneself, but also one's family, up the social scale" (Mauss 2002: 47–8). Thus, the potlatch of the

Kwakiutl reveals another aspect of the symbolic dimension of the things given, namely, social status and power; power entails the ability to reciprocate the given potlatch with an equal or more extravagant one.

Furthermore, several studies can be found to support the thesis that trade has its origins in the symbolic exchange of gifts. Weber (1981: 197) makes the point that trade grew out of gifts, and stresses that the exchange of goods in archaic societies has its origins in magical purposes and does not underlie the formal laws of rational exchange and modern economic activity. Gifts establish social relations and result in trust, an idea supported by, for example, studies of Vikings (Skre 2007) and of "traditional" economies (Bourdieu 1977; Malinowski 1922; Polanyi 1957a: 256–63; Thurnwald 1969: 149).

Gifts thus reflect a common interest, in contrast to the conflicting interests of trade, which is characterized by struggle. It is wrong to view gifts as embedded, since the point is that they were never unembedded.[2] Embeddedness presupposes difference between action and culture, and exactly this was never the case in a non-differentiated society, in contrast to what we have known since the advent of the modern era. The actions Malinowski describes were an inseparable part of a larger whole, guided by religious conceptions. Thus, all actions, including what we today call "economic," used to be guided by what Comte called "theological" or "fictitious" interpretations of the world. Out of gifts grew the idea of more systematic gift exchange, which later developed into barter. This may have occurred when gift exchanges began to be accompanied by the statement that implies: "if I get A you get B." This increased the match between the gifts and would have represented a distinct stage of "development" from a pure gift economy to an economy of barter. In this light, we can understand trade, which can facilitate more complex deals, as a form of systematization of barter. Monetary trade allows one to show up with money instead of goods at the trading place (Thurnwald 1969: 141).

If trade grew out of gift and gift exchanges, can we also date this change? The existence of trade, at least in its rudimentary forms, may be traceable to the Neolithic period (8500 BC), and Polanyi

(1957c) argues that there is clear evidence of what he calls market-less trading around 1800 BC. Price-making markets, in contrast, "were to all accounts non-existent before the first millennium of antiquity" (Polanyi 1957a: 257). As we have indicated, the first steps toward a market with a clear competitive structure may have been taken when enough traveling traders were around at a given time to enable the farmers and other customers to clearly compare prices and the quality of what was being offered. This can be seen as a forerunner of markets. Later, when several of them came together in "cities," met at certain places, or when they traveled together, a proper market may have been formed. Polanyi is thus probably correct when he says that the origin of markets appears not to be local markets (Polanyi 2001: 59–70), but long-distance trade or, more specifically, traveling traders, as suggested above. This idea is supported by Geertz, who sees the driving force of economic development in Java as "neither local trade not local manufacture . . . but long distance, ultimately inter-national, trade" (Geertz 1963: 42–3). North (2003: 434) identifies a number of long-distance markets in the fifth century BC. It is, according to this argument, the "division of labor" determined by the geographical location of groups rather than the division of labor between individuals that is the origin of trade and markets (Polanyi 2001: 61; Weber 1981: 198).

It is unclear in what form the first markets appeared. One example of an early form of market place is the Agora in ancient Athens, although our knowledge of it is limited (Thompson and Wycherley 1972). The Agora was a religious, political, and public place where people met: "the Athenian going to buy goods (ago-razein) here might say he was going to the Agora, no less than he was attending a political meeting" (Thompson and Wycherley 1972: 171). The Agora already constituted a highly institution-alized form of market, with rules, courts, defined boundaries, market booths, and so on (Swedberg 2003: 136–7; Thompson and Wycherley 1972). The Agora in ancient Athens appears to be an early form of market in which specialized merchants offered goods of different kinds, such as wine, fish, greens, garlic, or pots (Thompson and Wycherley 1972: 171). Goods were often imported by long-distance trade. For example, wine was imported from the sixth century BC up to the sixth century AD (Thompson and Wycherley 1972: 172). There is evidence of quality and price differentiation of wine; most of the wine was moderately priced, from Rhodes and Knidos, but high-quality and costly wines from Chios, Thasos, and Mende were also offered from time to time. We can also learn something about the formation and organization of early markets from the Agora: "The activities of the market were kept under some degree of state control through the board of ago-ranomoi and more specialized officials such as the sitophykakes (corn inspectors) and metronomoi [Commissioners of Weights and Measures]" (Thompson and Wycherley 1972: 172). Also, other economies, such as the Viking economy, show clear evidence of trading sites (Hedeager 1994). In the early eighth century, well-organized markets existed, especially for products that could not form part of the still dominant gift economy (Hedeager 1994: 138–9).

Though the market has extension in time, this does not mean that trading places were permanent. The fair was one early market form, held on certain dates and in particular places, which for this reason can be called a periodic market (Eighmy 1972; Park 1981; cf. Thurnwald 1969: 162), when traders came to a specific place. There was even a mobile labor market (Braudel 1982: 116–17; cf. Jeggle 2009).

This trading must be understood in relation to the existence of extensive trading circuits. We know that later, from the fifteenth to the eighteenth centuries, intercontinental trading circuits were important for market exchange (Braudel 1992: 138–54). Merchants could participate in two-way or triangular circuits, in which goods were exchanged for other goods or money. The most important aspect for a merchant on a circuit was security, guarantees that the circuit would be successfully completed (Braudel 1992: 144). If a merchant could not complete the trade circuit, the result would often be huge losses, meaning bankruptcy for some. Therefore, when a circuit could not be completed or could not be completed in a certain period of time, it was doomed to vanish. For example, the Frankfurt fair suffered greatly from the suspension of trade between France and Holland in 1793 (Braudel 1992: 145). This example reveals the importance of security, stability, and trust in early trade. Since the most profitable business of the time consisted of long-distance journeys to the West Indies and the Indian Ocean, the importance of security and trust for the merchant seems obvious. But how could these resources be allocated at a time when international rules such as the modern *lex mercatoria*, which is enforceable and applicable through national and international organizations (Volckart and Mangels 1999), did not exist?

Braudel points to trading networks as key institutions that provided information and trust beyond national borders: "Any commercial network brought together a certain number of individuals or agents, whether belonging to the same firm or not, located at different points on a circuit or a group of circuits. Trade thrived on these communications, on the cooperation and connections which automatically flowered with the increasing property of the interested parties" (Braudel 1992: 149). This suggests that institutions and networks constitute the bedrock of commercial exchange, which supports what Durkheim and many others have observed: trust is prior to trade and the idea of establishing relations by signing contracts.

Furthermore, there was a strict code among merchants and the use of agents was essential for providing information that was important for the deal. Thus, the codes between merchants and feudal lords were essential for the construction of trust and security for cross-border trading activities. For example, in Seville and Cadiz – the important Spanish ports to America – the underworld was notorious and corruption and fraud were the order of the day. But there was a "professional code," a network of solidarity between the merchants and the agents, which made cross-border collaboration possible; local agents knew the informal rules, how to act, how to talk, and what to offer the local authorities to ensure secure transmission of goods to the ships. Of course, these networks also made illegal business, such as smuggling, possible:

> The Dutch were, from the late sixteenth century, regularly and with impunity using go-betweens as front men for placing their cargoes

on board the Spanish fleets and bringing back the counterpart from America. Everyone in Cadiz knew the metedores (smugglers and runners) [...] Taking risks and living flamboyant lives, they were looked down on by respectable society, but were whole hearted participants in a system of solidarities which was the very backbone of this trading city. (Braudel 1992: 152–3)

It should be added that these cross-border trading networks gave rise to the development of ethnic trading networks. The most prominent examples of this are smaller ethnic groups, such as the Armenians and the Jews, who expanded all over the world, especially in the Middle East, Europe, and, later, the United States (Braudel 1992: 154–60).

Generally speaking, merchants belonging to minorities – either by nationality or by religion – often controlled trade (Jews, Armenians, Banyans, Parsees, the Raskolniki in Russia, and the Christian Copts in Muslim Egypt) (Braudel 1992: 165). Braudel's explanation for this is, to some extent, a sociological one: a minority sticks together for mutual aid and defense: "A minority, in other terms, was a solid and ready-made network" (Braudel 1992: 167). One should not forget the large trading empires, such as those of Italy or Holland, but from a historical point of view it is clear that all these networks had their peak and then declined: "All networks, even the most solid, sooner or later encountered difficulty or misfortune" (Braudel 1992: 167). The sociological interpretation is that, although networks are efficient, they are by definition not manageable, unless turned into organizations.

It is also in terms of networks that we can interpret some of the early signs of global trade. Ethnic networks settled all over the world and helped to stabilize and carry on the development of the market: "In Germany which had lost most of its capitalist merchants with the Thirty Year's War, a vacuum had been created which was filled by Jewish traders at the end of the seventeenth century, their rise being visible quite early, at the Leipzig fairs for example" (Braudel 1992: 159).

Another point which should be stressed is the development of the legal system governing markets. Its origins can be found in the

medieval *lex mercatoria*, the "Law of Merchants," which played
a crucial role in the provision of trust and security in a "world of
high danger and insecurity" (Volckart and Mangels 1999: 14).
According to Volckart and Mangels, there is no indication that
cross-border trade increased during the ninth and tenth centuries,
although what we call "merchants" in the classical sense did exist.
These merchants practiced very unspecialized trade, however.
During the Carolingian age (fifth to ninth centuries AD), the role
of the merchant changed; their status increased and they were able
to obtain more and more autonomy, in contrast to their previous
social position as mere agents of secular or ecclesiastical landlords.
During the "commercial revolution" in the eleventh century, the
occupation of merchant experienced a historic breakthrough.
Volckart and Mangels (1999) argue that the main basis for this
revolution consisted of new ways of ensuring security against
plunderers and raiders, thereby boosting trust in trade.

The main instrument was the formation of "guilds" to protect
the property of merchants. It is important to stress that these guilds
had little in common with the cartelistic fraternities of the later
Middle Ages; these guilds were "genuine protective co-operatives,"
and "communities of mutual trust" (cf. Commons 1909; Volckart
and Mangels 1999: 16). In addition, guilds were social platforms
on which merchants could build up reputation and status: a merchant's social status was high if he was considered, for example,
honorable, honest or powerful. When a merchant was suspected
of violating the social code of trade, the guild also had the function
of dispute settlement: "The exclusion of offenders was in the interest of every honest merchant" (Volckart and Mangels 1999: 20). It
is important to emphasize that exclusion from the guild could have
dire consequences for a merchant: "today, a loss of reputation just
means a loss of opportunities to do business. At the close of the
Dark Ages, it additionally meant exclusion from the community
which provided physical security: the affected merchant had to
fend for himself under conditions which approached anarchy"
(Volckart and Mangels 1999: 20). Thus, these guilds fulfilled the
pioneer function of what later would be the function of the state:
the provision of trust and security.

The second phase of the "commercial revolution" accompanied the rise of urbanization during the twelfth and thirteenth centuries. When the guilds lost their archaic constitutions, they could no longer maintain the right not to have to pay customs and generally lost their authority and privileges, their rights subsequently being granted to all merchants. This new and comprehensive system of rights constituted the *ius mercatorum* (*ius* having the meaning of "right" in this instance). The term first occurred in 1290 and contributed to the social construction of the merchant as a member of a system of rights and privileges, which distinguished him from the rest of the population. In the enforcement of urban law by civic councils, the guiding principle known as *forum contractus* became institutionalized. *Forum contractus* implied the "competence of the court of law of the town where a contract had been concluded" (Volckart and Mangels 1999: 28). Thus, it was reasonable for merchants to formulate their contracts in the towns where they would meet. In addition to the *forum contractus*, towns provided courts where disputes about trade and contracts could be settled (Volckart and Mangels 1999: 28).

The guilds had an interest in controlling and monopolizing not only production, but also trade, to reduce competition (Polanyi 2001: 67–8). Furthermore, guild members and other actors who were permanently located in towns made it possible to conduct trade which was not just simultaneous, such as barter. The extension of credit and commercial enterprises over time and to different places also increased the role of trade law that was the same in all markets, regardless of their location.

We will follow Volckart and Mangels, who argue that the legal system of the Middle Ages cannot be directly compared to the modern *lex mercatoria*. But it is interesting for a sociological history of markets to follow the development of pre-modern legal systems and to inquire how they helped to develop the framework for a system of trade. It is thus important to see the connection between commodity markets, the need for credit, and the legal structure. Within this legal structure, we can more easily understand why trade in markets is peaceful (Weber 1978).

To understand the transaction cost economics approach of

Volckart and Mangels, it is important to analyze the dimension of politics and power, which had a significant impact on stability in the historical development of pre-modern markets. As already pointed out, a permanent market place in which actors could come together and exchange goods was preferable as trade grew and there was a growing demand for predictable access to goods. Moreover, the dangers of travel in medieval Europe promoted organized transportation and permanent places of trade, and sovereigns could offer protection to those in transit and security within their fortifications. In return, merchants had to pay customs and protection fees. To hold a market was either something that a sovereign could decide or a right he could grant (cf. Skre 2007: 453). Holding a market was, in a way, constitutive of being a sovereign as it also meant revenue from taxation (Weber 1998: 163). Weber says that "princes . . . wished to acquire taxable dependents and therefore founded towns and markets" (Weber 1981: 132). In England, for example, markets were allowed only if the Crown had granted the right to trade and to hold a market, as records from the mid-eleventh century show (Britnell 1978). Such rights reflect the Crown's need for income from taxation (Britnell 1978: 189). It was, however, possible for the Crown in England to transfer the right to "hold a market" to private persons, which is a form of "franchise" (Masschaele 1992). Consequently, we can say that the organization of secure trading places and – most importantly – the need for tax revenue meant that markets were regulated and organized directly by princes and other sovereigns. Moreover, markets, or more accurately their organizers, competed with each other for merchants and for access to tax revenues.

Over time, markets came to be controlled by councils residing in the cities, instead of by a single sovereign (Glamann 1977; Weber 1981: 214). The organization of markets is likely to have increased with the appearance of market towns and, later, when market halls were built (Braudel 1992: 33). Furthermore, travelers needed food, shelter, and other kinds of support, which called for additional "market activities," offered by those who resided in the market town permanently. There is often – although not always – a close connection between the emergence of cities and of markets

(Weber 1978: 114). However, anthropologists have shown that informal forms of market existed before we can talk of a state in any modern sense (Dalton and Bohannan 1971), which of course is also true of markets in Europe.

Organization and standardization

It was only on the basis of a stable social order, and with the establishment of trading places, standards of trade, goods and legal principles with validity in a larger area, that certificates could fully replace transactions with goods. Standardization of what was traded is thus of great importance. Originally, samples were brought by sellers to buyers, who only then decided whether to buy or not. In this case, shipment of the batch followed later. In such a situation, not only the offers were important, but who was making the offer. Later, goods were standardized, including measurements, such as length and weight. This standardization was also the condition for trading in the rights to goods, as in stock exchanges (Weber 1981: 293). Standardization meant that the goods did not have to be physically present, as at the fair. The stock exchange in Amsterdam, arguably the first stock exchange, appears to have been set up by the city authorities, reacting to the exchange of rights that was already going on in the city. The first stock to be traded – in 1602 – was the East India Company in Amsterdam, which needed investors to finance its long-distance operations. Trading rights and shares, but also futures, requires standardized products. Obviously, standardization is not enough; market institutions also had to be developed in order that a market could replace the direct trading of goods at fairs and market places.

Stock exchanges, as in Stockholm or Brussels, are often located in the city center, which was important when trading was still personal. The centrality of the market, and the interconnection of market making and town making, can be seen in historical maps of cities. The Agora in Athens and the Forum in Rome are early examples of this, but similar observations can be made in many old cities, such as Istanbul, Cologne, and Brussels. An even larger sample would merely reinforce the tendency toward the centrality of the market place, namely, in the town square.

These above-mentioned examples do not show that markets were originally the product of organized efforts, but they do suggest that markets were developed against the backdrop of a lifeworld of institutions and trust. They also suggest that markets were put in place to facilitate trade or, more explicitly, to obtain tax revenues. Many of the markets we know of were, as indicated, to some extent organized. Maitland agrees, concluding that "the market is established by law," going on to say that this "prohibits men from buying and selling elsewhere than in a duly consti-tuted market" (Maitland 1907: 193). Polanyi speaks, in a similar fashion, of the "double function of the towns with regard to the markets which they both enveloped and prevented from develop-ing" (Polanyi 2001: 65). Trade, in other words, became controlled to prevent trade being conducted outside market places and to provide an income for those holding the rights to trade (Weber 1978: 1328–31).

From this historical perspective, it is clear that the development of the market is tied to a process of increased order over time. The complex phenomena of the modern market cannot be understood as a process of rational and atomized actors attaining their ends. The study of history and anthropology reveals the social and sym-bolic dimensions of exchange that tie actors together and create order, only given this context of an ordered lifeworld is "rational" action possible as one style (White 2008) among others (Pareto 1935). With ordered market elements over time, more complex social formations became possible, which means today we can talk of a "market economy" of several related markets. Next we turn to the question of how this market economy could develop, which means looking at the context in which markets were embedded.

Differentiation of Spheres of Life

The development of markets and the theories pertaining to them, which are the focus of this book, should not prevent us from noticing another central effect in society, namely, that the economy gradually developed its own logic. This process is not identical to market society, but it is clearly correlated with it, since markets are engines of change. Furthermore, the separate and autonomous sphere that we call the economy, and that is often seen as the sole subject matter of economics, is of a more recent date than the oldest references to the term. We should understand the difference between spheres of life and what we today take for granted, capitalist markets, as two correlated processes. The differentiation of spheres of life, with their own meaning and justification of actions, accounts for the ethical legitimacy of markets (Zelizer 1979).

Max Weber (1946: 323–31, 333–57) argued that all the different spheres of life, each with a certain autonomy (*Eigengesetzlichkeit*), have emerged out of the religious sphere. The economic sphere is characterized by instrumental rationality, impersonal exchange, depersonalization, objectification, universal measures, calculation, and formal contracts. The values of this sphere may conflict with those of other spheres. We will give a brief account of the well-known story of the origin of the spirit of rational capitalism, as explained by Weber (1968). The change in the capitalist spirit, Weber says, was caused by individuals who had internalized the spirit of capitalism. These people did business in a different way, which resulted, we presume, in a better match between customer demand and the commodities produced. This forced other business owners, due to competition, to "go with the flow" or withdraw from business. The capitalist system is not, according to Weber, a consequence of planned actions toward a well-defined end. It is rather the outcome of individuals' actions that are oriented to religious values or virtues. This social process meant that a different value base was established for the separate sphere that came to be called the economic sphere. The separate science of "economics," which studies the economy, is, of course, of much later date (Foucault 2002).

It is only with the gradual separation of spheres of life that we can talk of "the economy" as something driven by its own logic. Polanyi's (1957b) discussion should be seen in light of a modern society that increasingly is coordinated by means of the market. It is this effect that he and others – such as Marx, Simmel, Weber, Marshall, Pareto, Durkheim, and Habermas – analyzed. They all stressed the dangerous development of the human condition. Money (Carruthers 2005) penetrated other forms of interaction (Habermas 1984; Luhmann 1988).

Capitalism

Clearly, there is a strong correlation between capitalism and markets. Today we may talk of forms of capitalism in China, Russia, and many other economies, but this is only one phase in a long development. Capitalism has been an unprecedented engine of growth, as already noted by Marx. Though many countries in the West of the twentieth century have combined capitalism with freedom and democracy, this is no necessary relation, neither today nor in history. While some would say that we live in a capitalist society, they are, strictly speaking, wrong. Social life as a whole has never been capitalistic, although a large part of it is. We can observe, by looking at almost all definitions of the economy, that only a few of them refer to capitalistic economies (Braudel 1992: 231ff).

The differentiation of the economic sphere was a condition of the development of rational capitalism. The core of modern Western rational capitalism is rooted in values. This is clear in the classical Weberian analysis. Weber says that the spirit of capitalism is "a duty of the individual toward the increase of his capital, which is assumed as an end in itself" (Weber 1968: 51). The ultimate end is to make money for its own sake, which he says is the "result and expression of virtue and proficiency in a calling" (Weber 1968: 54). Weber defines a (rational) capitalistic action "as one which rests on the expectation of profit by the utilization of opportunities for exchange, that is on (formally) peaceful chances of profit" ([1904–5] 1968: 17). One important aspect of capitalistic actions is the market, which is a precondition for rational calculation.

Capitalism, Weber argues, means that money becomes an end in itself. This has fundamentally changed the values of society. One consequence is that people not only make some money, and then settle down, but also accumulate money and reinvest it in industry, thereby triggering additional economic development. Weber argues that rational industrial capitalism only emerged in the Western world, and this is part of his general argument about the rationalization of the West. "The decisive impetus toward capitalism," Weber says, "could come only from one source, namely a mass market demand, which again could arise only in a small proportion of the luxury industries through the democratization of the demand, especially along the line of production of substitutes for the luxury goods of the upper classes" (1981: 310). Hence, Weber stresses the importance of both consumption and markets for the development of capitalism. Today, capitalistic values are deeply entrenched cultural values.

Marketization

To understand marketization we must look at the combined effect of capitalism and differentiated spheres of life. Marketization refers to the process in which markets and, more generally, market logic have been diffused in social life. To answer the question of how markets have become so prevalent in social life, we must look at the political and cultural structure. By looking at the role of power, we can see how market activities can be promoted or blocked. We must also look at what markets enable people to do, due to the power of economic means of its possessors, as well as what this situation does to people.

It would, in principle, be possible to have a single organization to take care of all decisions in society, but historically this is not what we observe. Our historical overview has suggested some answers to the question of market dominance. One is that markets were developed by economic actors as the level of generalized trust, largely due to the growth and stability of institutions and personal networks, increased in society. But states have also fostered and cultivated markets, and have turned market exchanges outside the state into legal transactions in order to increase their tax revenues. The bureaucratic need of states to finance their armies was one strong reason why the factory system and then the mass market developed (cf. Commons 1909: 73). But it is not clear to what extent markets are the result of political processes or whether it is the other way around.

Markets allow actors freedom and, with increased wealth – which markets are both the cause and effect of – there is a corresponding weakening of personal ties of dependence. Market interaction, moreover, made it possible for people to obtain identities that were not merely derivations of the clan or family. Durkheim's (1984) study of solidarity in light of economic development is a good example of a sociological work showing how social relations change with a more market-oriented society. Durkheim, who followed up on Adam Smith's discussion of the division of labor, argued that the solidarity in primitive societies is a result of people being engaged in similar activities (mechanical solidarity). In more modern societies, where people's tasks are different but interconnected, one person depends on another who does something else. This form of solidarity he called organic solidarity. The division of labor and production for markets, and not for specific and known users, depersonalizes relations between people, which also is a theme in the writings of Simmel. We can say that the market contributes to individualism and more shallow interpersonal relations, but it also enables such kinds of relations. It is a moral imperative to find the right balance between the forces of individuality and collectivity (Simmel 1923).

Markets are just one form of social interaction in which people can establish relations with people and things, which enables personal expression. More generally, consumption, which is intimately related to markets, has enabled people to make distinctions (Veblen 1953). The expansion of markets cannot be reduced to a simple cause or effect of the marketization process. It is because of the ongoing activities conducted by people who are forward-looking – such as the businessperson who invests money loaned by another investor in opening up a small shop, in the hope (Swedberg 2005a) that this will incur profit – that expansion can be understood. This kind of sequence of interdependent actions, each of which supports (or destroys) the conditions of others, takes place because of the actors' hope for a better future, in the widest sense of the word, but also because of faith in the institutional framework that embed actors. Ordered markets are crucial here. Though other coordination forms are possible, and indeed necessary for ordered markets to come about, markets seems to be a highly efficient coordination form in a large number of cases.

The more efficiency becomes the value used for evaluating different coordination forms, the more likely it is that the market will be the decided outcome. Hayek points in a similar direction when he argues that we must look at information-processing capacity and price signaling when we want to understand the "superiority of the market order, and the reason why, when it is not suppressed by the powers of the government, it regularly displaces other types of order" (Hayek 1975: 436). Although these reasons could indeed be put forward, history tells us that this "superiority" is not the given value for evaluating the most preferable form of coordination. Furthermore, from the large literature in the political economy tradition that has stressed the great variety of capitalisms, it is clear that a pure market society does not have to do better than a more state-centered one (Hall and Soskice 2001). However, the efficiency of the form of coordination does not tell us much about the consequences for citizenship and democratic rights. We now turn to these broader questions.

Social consequences and capitalism

One central question regarding markets concerns the consequences of market diffusion. The debate is well over 300 years old and should be related not only to the spread of markets, but also to the spread of capitalism. Although it is possible to separate the normative standpoint on markets from the positive analysis of markets in society, many participants in the debate have brought them close to one another. This is not surprising since economics as we know it today grew out of political economy, with clear origins in ethics. Some thinkers, such as Aristotle, can be interpreted as saying that ethical reasoning is not relevant to such *trivial* questions as economics. Few today would agree.

Marketization – and its positive and negative consequences – is the main theme in Albert Hirschman's essay "Rival Views of Market Society" (Hirschman 1986). Here it is enough to reconstruct the two main positions, which nonetheless stress the role of the market. The so-called *doux-commerce* ("gentle business") thesis suggests that "the market and capitalism were going to create a moral environment in which society as well as the market itself were bound to flourish" (Hirschman 1986: 135). More practically, commerce and social interaction between people doing business with each other would lead to virtues and, eventually, a better society in terms of economic and social wealth (and order). This idea was stressed by Mandeville (1924) and Adam Smith (1981). Among neoliberals (Nozick 1974), the old idea of laissez-faire has been esteemed. Marshall informs us about the origins of laissez-faire. He says that "its original meaning was that guilds and *métiers* should not prohibit people from entering a trade for which they were competent; any one should be at liberty to choose his own work: Let Government keep up its police, but in other matters go to sleep" (Marshall 1907: 18). It was, consequently, only later that laissez-faire became associated with opposition to the state, ideas developed by Smith and others, who lived in a time when the state was routinely corrupt. Much later, we find similar arguments among the Austrian school, who also reacted against socialism (Hayek 1973, 1976, 1988; Mises 1981). One corollary is taxation, and the discussion of what to be taxed and to what extent.

While there has been a strong movement since at least the 1980s criticizing the role of the state and praising the self-regulation of markets, others have stressed the negative consequences of markets and capitalism, usually arguing that the values praised in the market invade other spheres of life (Habermas 1984). The latter is the typical sociological point of view, which has been echoed many times since Marx's early formulations, the key idea being capitalistic market societies generate the values which eventually will destroy the foundations on which this market logic rests. The founding fathers of sociology wrote about marketization, rationalization, and economization. Marx, Weber, and Durkheim went for the big picture, but it was Simmel who honed in on the details. Simmel (1978) studied the effects of competition, and he saw how this, combined with the value of money, affected social life, especially when every other value was reduced to money.

The discussion of capitalism is too vast to cover here, especially since it is well known in the sociological literature (Bell 1979; Greenfeld 2001; Schumpeter 1975; Swedberg 2005c; Trigilia 2002; Zelizer 2005a). Many sociologists have had a mixed opinion about market capitalism. And, of course, the most influential critic of capitalistic market logic, Karl Marx, also saw the enormous wealth generated by the market capitalistic stage (Marx 1978), although he never used the term "capitalism." Marx's historical perspective revealed uneven distribution of resources between the classes in the different forms of society, from the first social formations to the advanced capitalist society of nineteenth-century Northern Europe. The labor market was for Marx the arena of exploitation. It was in this market that value was generated by workers in factories, but, according to Marx, they were not paid their full share of the value they created. The portion they did not get, and which was kept by the capitalist, was exploited by the latter. The consequence is that wealth is accumulated by capitalists at the expense of workers. According to Marx, this conflict of interest would eventually lead to revolution and the abolition of capitalism. Marx indeed inspired people to social action, and the introduction of communism can to some extent be attributed to his writings.

Several sociologists since Marx have identified and developed critical ideas about market capitalism (Fevre 2003). The debate on capitalism was originally harsh, but capitalist society has proved able to survive major crises, in the 1930s and, more recently, in 2008, although some have blamed "the market" for these failures. Alex Preda (2009) has shown in a historical study of finance how financial markets – which are at the heart of the capitalist economy – have gradually acquired systemic importance. Some financial institutions have become so central that, in the crisis of

2008 and 2009, states across the world made sure, by offering guarantees, loans, or simply taking them over, that they did not fail.

Even at the advent of the most severe financial crisis since the 1930s, few have changed their perception of the market system as being the best option, although it is hard to find people who see it as perfect. In fact, the thesis that markets are necessarily embedded has gained ground. Markets need institutions, both formal and informal, in order to function. These markets have partly to be created, although there are few recipes. The view that markets are efficient but need a social context is, for example, held by Amitai Etzioni: "Similarly, competition is beneficial as long as it is properly embedded in a supportive societal context, which ensures that the prerequisites of competition are met while limiting its scope" (Etzioni 1988: 10).

Amitai Etzioni (Etzioni 1988) intends nothing less than to offer *the* revolutionary critique of the paradigm's fundamentals that will lead to its dissolution. The basic set of neoclassical assumptions is criticized and enlarged by references to deontological ethics, a more communitarian relationship between society and individual, with power structures as coordination devices. He proposes a clearly normative alternative, which is "moderately deontological" (1988: 253), to the neoclassical theory he criticizes. Karl Polanyi is another thinker who has had a major impact on critical social scientific ideas on markets. But it is clear that his work has had a significant impact on the current debate on markets and the economy more generally (e.g., Gemici 2008; Hann and Hart 2009).

Marketization and functional differentiation

We have so far discussed marketization and social change at a fairly abstract level, and in general terms. But what does it mean? To show in more detail how this process works, its causes as well as what it may cause, let us turn to a more detailed study. John Common's (1909) study, based on documentation on American shoemakers from 1648 to 1895, is an excellent example of how activities in this industry have gradually become marketized, a process that goes hand in hand with the division of labor and specialization, as described by Adam Smith (1981) and Émile Durkheim (1984). Commons focuses on how market actors join together and organize themselves. The different organizations he describes reflect the structure of the market, although these organizations of course also structure markets. The organization is of intrinsic interest, as it clearly shows that actors who at one level are competitors, at another level can collaborate to further their common interests.

Before Commons's chosen starting point, in the mid-seventeenth century, shoemakers traveled, using their tools to make shoes from materials provided by buyers, in the homes of the latter. Later, these travelers returned home to their small workshops to finish the work. According to Commons, the American shoemaking industry in the mid-seventeenth century was controlled by masters and their associates, and the guild was the prevalent organizational form. Commons says that the primary aim of the members was to control quality so that each of them was a "sufficient workman" (Commons 1909: 41), and the workers were organized in guilds. The guild also had the right to regulate the work of its members. The legitimacy of the guild was laid down by law, that is, the state. In fact, it was almost a "branch of government" (Commons 1909: 41). This traveler was, in one person, merchant, master, and journeyman, and later these roles began to be separated among several hands, and market interaction between the functions became a central means of coordination. The differentiation of roles also meant that power was distributed between the sides of the markets that came into being by virtue of the emerging roles. This meant that producers could shift costs on to the consumers. It was in this process of marketization that employers and trade unions were formed (Commons 1909: 45). The masters of Philadelphia formed an organization in 1789 with the purpose of "taking into consideration the many inconveniencies which they labor under, for want of proper regulations among them, and to provide remedies for the same" (Commons 1909: 47). It is not difficult to see how such a statement could soon be turned into action, and this market organized accordingly. The organization controlled quality and eliminated competition from cheap products, as well as competition among masters, for example, by means of bargains. To become a member of the masters' organization required that the applicant had behaved well in the market, and qualification for membership was defined negatively: "No person shall be elected a member of this society who offers for sale any boots, shoes, &c., in the public market of this city, or advertises the prices of his work, in any of the public papers or hand-bills, so long as he continues in these practices" (Commons 1909: 47).

The major impact the labor unions have had on the three pre-requisites of markets we have identified – what is sold (regulation of what people sell in the labor market), how parties behave in the market, as well as how economic value (the wage) and the cost of shoes are determined – should be seen in this organizational light. This early organization of not only the employers, but also the workers, reflects the fundamental conflict of interests that char-acterizes markets. Strikes, on which Commons reports, form the concrete evidence of the struggle in markets between buyers and sellers.

Furthermore, in the late eighteenth century, each city was a market in its own right. Gradually, however, competition between markets – or, more accurately, sellers in different markets, which could be members of different organizations – became common. This form of struggle was not restricted to price; quality and ways of doing business were also contested. Some cities offered higher quality; others, lower prices. It was, Commons tells us, the com-petitive struggle in the market that caused organizations to split into the "modern alignment of employers' associations and trade unions" (Commons 1909: 50).

We cannot follow the details of Common's analysis, but it shows how new roles, such as merchant capitalist in the early nineteenth century (Commons 1909: 63), and corresponding organizations emerge. This leads to new markets and also the dif-ferentiation of markets. It is the merchant capitalist who creates "the antagonism of 'capital and land'" by forcing separation of functions (Commons 1909: 63). This is done by keeping informed of distant markets and making use of this knowledge – becoming a structural entrepreneur in the sense of Ronald Burt (1992), by not primarily organizing change, but making use of the superior knowledge available to someone who is "in" several markets. One consequence is that former employers have to find employment and capitalism forces workers to compete. Also the "merchant-function," which at first was functionally separated, later became separated into three different parts: custom merchant, retail merchant, and wholesale merchant – corresponding to the three levels of market competition. An essential aspect is the conflict of interest that this differentiation and marketization gave rise to; this we know not only from Commons, but also from Marx and Weber. An equally important aspect is that the markets were organized in both an informal and a formal sense, since virtually all "functions" were organized.

Out of the original market, in which "the producer is the seller to the consumer" (Commons 1909: 65), we have seen that capitalist logic grows, and specialization and functional differentiation go hand in hand with marketization. This also means that complexity increases, and actors react with an attempt to control the environment by ordering it to suit their interests. Commons also describes how the notion of quality, which was the first principle of evaluation – since only shoes of a certain quality were allowed to be produced – gradually turned people's attention to price. Competition further increases as a result of spatial expansion of a market; what used to be different, essentially separate, markets, each controlled by a separate guild, gradually became one market. But this process did not take place without organized struggle. Commons (1909: 69–71) shows how organized efforts were made to control quality and ward off low wages. However, there is no room here to follow Commons's account in detail.

Commons's study ends in 1895, but extrapolating his approach seems reasonable. This would allow us to interpret contemporary expansion in the shoemaking industry, with its global market and brands such as Nike and Adidas competing fiercely, not least by sponsoring athletes and soccer players. Production of sports shoes is no longer mainly done where the shoes are designed, in the

United States and Germany, but in low-wage countries all over the world. This is not only the case for sports shoes, but for all kinds of shoes. The global producer market is well in evidence in such industrial districts as Agra in India (Knorringa 1995).

Market Ideology

What are the consequences of markets for society, not primarily in the economic sense and measured in terms of efficiency, but in a social and moral sense (e.g., Durkheim 1984; Hirschman 1986; Simmel 1978, 1983; Stehr, Henning, and Weiler 2006)? It is possible to go further and to analyze several of the consequences and implications of marketization, and the so-called market society (Aldridge 2005; Slater and Tonkiss 2001). It is only as a result of the differentiation of the economy and the nascent capitalistic market society that the issue of specific consequences of market society can become an issue at all. In this section we will look briefly at the arguments for and against market society. This will take us into ideological debates, much of which can be reduced to two principal values. Supporters of the market and market capitalism as a way of arranging production, consumption, and distribution have often argued that it is the most efficient system, which generates the best overall outcome. Those criticizing market capitalism as an economic coordination system have argued that it does not lead to equality, and that it destroys other values.

We have already made it clear that many of the premises are problematic, including the starting point of rational actors who somehow "sign contracts" to solve all the coordination problems of the economy – and society at large – from scratch, based on their maximization of utility, according to their preferences. We should keep this in mind, and it is reasonable from a sociological point of view not to become preoccupied with such economistic problems and their consequences, as they appear only within the framework of theory and may sometimes be of less relevance in seeking to understand empirical problems.

Most economists have been in favor of market solutions, while sociologists have been more skeptical. But the ideological discussion transcends the question of markets. In other words, to focus only on the market is too narrow. Markets, we have said, are about the exchange of rights under competition. Property rights are primary and the role of the state is reduced to protection of such rights. Property rights and ownership, values, solidarity, and virtues are also of great importance. We have seen that ownership has gradually become personal and that the conception of trading rights is central in markets. Socialist doctrines, put forward most prominently by Marx, emphasize the value of collective ownership. The socialist argument must be seen, on the one hand, in light of the uneven distribution of power and resources in the many European societies in which capitalism has given rise not only to wealth creation, but also to redistribution and major social rupture. Socialists, on the other hand, have argued that the natural starting point is the community, in which property rights are not tied to individuals, but to the group.

Liberals have argued, furthermore, that there was a state of nature. According to Locke and other contract philosophers, private property is the result of human labor. Labor is put to use for appropriate resources from the land. This view essentially assumes a self-made person, who gradually creates resources. It is then assumed that people can freely trade what they have produced with others, as long as they do not extract resources that impinge on what others are doing, or affect the property rights of others. Liberals such as Hayek (1973, 1988) or Nozick (1974), but also many others, have stressed the importance of property rights and well-functioning – though often a limited number of – institutions, including the law (North 1990). Capitalism also has a number of academic supporters, such as Ludwig von Mises and Milton Friedman. They argue, in sum, that a deregulated market economy, with limited state involvement beyond securing basic rights and upholding the law, is the most efficient model for wealth production. Hayek's book *The Road to Serfdom* (1991) is a manifesto of this form of economic and political liberalism. These ideas of markets, as a form of the state of nature, are best seen as the consequence of man; this relation between human beings and the market is of central importance, and to this we now turn.

Economic Man and Social Man

Though this book focuses on markets, in both economics and sociology the dynamics of markets are strongly connected to which assumptions of man are used. In fact, we cannot understand market theories without looking more carefully into the assumptions of humanity that underlie these theories. What has not been noted is how the foundations of action theory in sociology and economics are surprisingly similar. The ideas of human action and the constitution used by economists – for example, Weber and Pareto – were taken over into sociology, but given a more sociological twist. Not only Pareto and Weber, but also Parsons, started out as economists, and all of them saw economic and social actions as different in kind. This historical mistake has led to much effort being expended in economic sociology, largely in vain, as we will soon see.

Man is both the starting and the end point of the economy. Economic actions occur in terms of coordination, market, network, and hierarchy (organization), but they can also have the purpose of creating one of these forms, such as when a company is started. These actions must be understood in relation to the ambiguity, uncertainty, and lack of information that are both characteristics and conditions of a dynamic economy. Uncertainty is not only a negative aspect; it is also systemically necessary for creating opportunities for action, and especially in the economy (Stark 2009).

It is through actions that human beings (which, given the relevant historical usage, it will sometimes be necessary to refer to simply as "man" – see below) solve their problems, and here we shall concentrate on markets. Humanity can solve the problems of production and consumption using various forms of coordination. But who is this "man"? In many theories – typically the action theories in anthropology, economics, and sociology – there is a human being who stands at the end, as the source of explanation.

This "actor," and the ontological, epistemological, and methodological assumptions of the theory in which he or she is a part, have ramifications for how problems are addressed and what counts as explanations.

The role of man in economic theory

The explanation of markets is a consequence of actors' *modus operandi*. Economists have proposed so-called economic man or *homo economicus*, who is in the market together with his identical peers, all of them signing contracts with each other, from which order emerges spontaneously. This idea has a long tradition: the Cartesian egological (referring to an atomistic and operating-in-solitude type of person) approach can be seen as its philosophical root and British utilitarianism as its principles of action. Although it was Pareto who first used the concept *homo oeconomicus*, the idea is older and arguably can be associated with John Stuart Mill (Ng and Tseng 2008: 266) and the maximization of "pleasure over pain" as a leading doctrine. This is the root of the rational choice approach, which essentially is a decision theory under scarcity (Hodgson 2007: 335) and has been turned into a set of assumptions about how actors operate. In other words, it is a normative theory which has been transformed into the core of how real actors behave in the economy.

Rational man has a set of preferences and acts more or less rationally to achieve goals. An important aspect of this is that it leads to isolation, and a person's preferences are, essentially, not affected by social interaction. Other sociologists, such as population ecologists (Park 1936), who have studied competition, niches, and markets extensively, have taken over a biological cousin of "economic man." Some economic sociologists also stress the role of "economic man," but in a quite different way, namely as a product of theory: "*homo oeconomicus* really does exist [. . .] he is obviously not found in a natural state [. . .] he is formatted, framed and equipped with prostheses which help him in his calculations and which are, <u>for the most part</u>, produced by economics" (Callon 1998a: 51).

The justification of economic man is muddy. Frank Knight (1921: 55–6) claims that, when we go back to "medieval times or to the American frontier, we find relatively little joint activity, except for the division of labor between the sexes and in the family." The atomistic and utilitarian anthropology of humanity represented in economics, in other words, is said to be universal (Knight 1921: 55). If one leaves this humanity to function unfettered, interaction with other egos will begin and this will result in the market. Oliver Williamson takes a similar, but more extreme view which also provides the context of economic man, informing us that, "In the beginning there were markets" (Williamson 1975: 20). This is not uncommon, and another Nobel laureate economist, Kenneth Arrow, also sees the market and its price mechanism as the starting point. Arrow asserts that "organizations are the means of achieving the benefits of collective action in situations in which the price system fails" (Arrow 1974: 33). The market and its accompanying price system, under perfect competition and full information, is the absolute starting point of economics, but does not need to be explained as it is the result of a natural process based on assumptions about economic man. It is also because of this assumption of the market as naturally evolving that the economists' contribution to research on markets is limited. Stigler admits that economists have done little to define markets, and says that

> [m]y lament is that this battle on market definitions, which is fought thousands of times what with all the private antitrust suits, has received virtually no attention from us economists. Except for a flirtation with cross elasticities of demand and supply, the determination of the market has remained an underdeveloped area of economic research at either the theoretical or empirical level. (Stigler 1982: 9)

What is in need of explanation, according to economists who defend this more neoclassical school, are the deviating cases, such as markets with imperfect competition.

Although Williamson, Arrow, and many other economists, if they were pushed, are less likely to see the market – and the set of assumptions on which its rests, such as full information – as the historically correct starting point, the market as an analytical starting point has created a number of "pseudo problems" (Withford 2002). Such issues, based on these assumptions, include free-riding (that is, where an actor benefits from the activities of others – collective activities and correlated resources – without contributing), and moral hazard (that is, the danger that a party to a contract who is thereby shielded from risk will behave differently), appear as problems only given certain assumptions about human beings. If all actors behaved according to the assumptions of the neoclassical market model, no state could have emerged and no markets could have been organized; we would only have a market in which actors were signing contracts with one another.

The so-called transaction cost approach, which Williamson (1975, 1981) has propagated and is rooted in the works of Coase (1937, 1988), stresses the role of contracts. The first ideas about contracts, however, are much older and are to be found in the work of Thomas Hobbes (1968). The transaction – the contract – is the starting point of analysis, and firms (hierarchies) exist to diminish transaction costs between individuals. The central problem, given the assumptions of a rational man who must coordinate his actions with an environment made up of other people, who also are "in the market," and resources which are securely possessed on the basis of accepted property rights, is the choice confronting market participants of either signing contracts, which goes together with "transaction costs," or deciding to set up an economic organization, in the form of a hierarchically organized firm, to coordinate activities within the hierarchy or, better, within an organization (Ahrne 1994). In the latter case, the market is put in parentheses. Williamson refers to Adam Smith's classical example of a pin-making factory to illustrate the division of labor, and argues that one could have each worker operating on the basis of contracts signed on markets with others in the technological production chain, but also says that this form of coordination could not handle eventualities such as becoming sick, not to mention penalties. He sees hierarchy as a solution to these and other dilemmas of market contract-based coordination (Williamson 1975: 50–1).

Thus, among economists, where one might expect to find a wealth of research on markets, the actual study of markets has been almost neglected. The economist Ronald Coase is explicit about this: "although economists claim to study the market, in modern economic theory the market itself has an even more shadowy existence than the firm"; he also says that "the discussion of the market itself has entirely disappeared" (1988: 7).

Critique of economic man

There are, of course, criticisms of economic man among economists. Herbert Simon's (1955) notion of bounded rationality, which refers to limitations on decision-makers' information and cognitive capacities, is one attempt to correct some of the assumptions. The external critique of economic man is old and strong, and not seldom "hostile." It would be easy to list all those who have criticized this creature. It suffices to give a few examples, as they tend to go in the same direction. Feminists have claimed that economic man lives a selfish life in the market, while at the same time being "the benign head of the household, who provides for his family and whose decisions are taken to reflect their general interest," as reported by Slater and Tonkiss (2001: 113). Veblen adds that

> The hedonistic conception of man is that of a lightning calculator of pleasures and pains, who oscillates like a homogeneous globule of desire of happiness under the impulse of stimuli that shift about the area, but leave him intact. He is an isolated, definitely human datum, in stable equilibrium except for the buffets of impinging forces that displaces him in one direction or another. (Veblen 1898: 389)

The social scientist Karl Polanyi spells out why the economic starting point leads us astray: "The individualistic savage [who is the root of economic man] collecting food and hunting on his own or for his family has never existed" (2001: 55). This argument is related to the general point of embeddedness: "The human economy, then, is embedded and enmeshed in institutions, economic and noneconomic" (Polanyi 1957a: 250). But Polanyi, in this case, only echoes the economic sociologist Malinowski who says the following about "economic man":

> This fanciful, dummy creature, who has been very tenacious of existence in popular and semi-popular economic literature, and whose shadow haunts even the minds of competent anthropologists, blighting their outlook with a preconceived idea, is an imaginary primitive man, or savage, prompted in all his actions by a rationalistic conception of self-interest, and achieving his aims directly with the minimum of effort. (Malinowski 1922: 60)

Malinowski claims that the Trobriand Islanders confound the theoretical construct of economics. But none of the three writers on this subject – Malinowski, Veblen, and Polanyi – is capable of theoretically replacing "economic man" with something else which could be used to build a rival *theory*. Although all theories imply a reduction of the complexity of reality, many think that economic man is not only too reductionist, but also a distorted way of reducing complexity in favor of pursuing modeling. It is, furthermore, a non-social starting point, as economic man is isolated (confirmed by the notion of a Robinson Crusoe economy). What do the sociologists have to offer?

Sociological theories of humanity

Max Weber's theory of action essentially assumes a non-social being, who occasionally is involved in social activities. Weber's definition of sociology and his discussion of action make it clear that social action is only a sub-category of actions. Weber can hold this position only if he assumes that human beings are essentially non-social.

> Sociology [. . .] is a science concerning itself with the interpretative understanding of social action [. . .] We shall speak of 'action' insofar as the acting individual attaches a subjective meaning to his behavior – be it overt or covert, omission or acquiescence. Action is 'social' insofar as its subjective meaning takes account of the behavior of others and is thereby oriented in its course. (Weber 1978: 4)

The argument here is not that Weber's definition of economic action, which builds on his definition of social action, is flawed, as he is clearly stressing the social dimensions. However, the problem is that Weber proceeds from a non-sociological starting point. There is a level of non-social actions, as suggested by economics.

But Weber is not alone in viewing humanity as essentially non-social. According to Vilfredo Pareto, "social action" (or illogical action) is a sub-category of rational (logical) actions (Pareto 1935). That Parsons, who builds on Weber and Pareto, and who, like them, started out in economics, was never able to cast off its spell is no surprise. He proposed a division of labor, suggesting that sociologists should study social values, some of which go into economic calculations (Withford 2002: 328–30).

Let us turn to the best-known example of economic action, Mark Granovetter's text on embeddedness (1985), which has become almost the manifesto of new economic sociology, known for its reintroduction of the idea of embedded actions. The story of "the social" as something that is added on to economic action is repeated. Social actions – or embedded actions – are, according to Granovetter, rational actions which are constrained or enabled by their social relations. Let it be clear that we do not want to diminish the value of Granovetter's work; it is without doubt a leading text in economic sociology. However, we want to move beyond the discussion of *homo sociologicus* and *homo economicus*, which has been central to economic sociology (Ng and Tseng 2008). The point here is that the economic sociological tradition has remained within an egological approach which starts out with rational actors.

Although it is clear that sociologists operate with a richer concept of "man," as discussed by Smelser and Swedberg (1994), there is little alternative to economic man. We agree with Greta Krippner, who is critical of the sociologically naive idea which some first-generation economic sociologists presented. The sharpest critique is directed toward the idea of the separation of the economy and the social. She shows that Granovetter, too, works with the idea of a non-social starting point (Krippner 2001: 777), which presupposes that the economy is a non-social domain. She also refers critically to Fred Block, who tends to see markets as "pure," although embedded in wider social networks (Krippner 2001: 784–5). She makes the important point that we must not be caught in the spell of economics if we want to advance economic sociology. It is important to say that the non-social foundation of sociology is a general problem that, hence, is not restricted to economic sociology. It must be noted, however, that leading economists, such as Alfred Marshall (1842–1924), clearly rejected the atomistic view. He said: "The individual should not be regarded as 'an isolated atom'", and this means that "[i]n all [such kinds of analysis] economists deal with man as he is: not with an abstract or 'economic' man; but a man of flesh and blood" (Marshall 1896: 40–1). Next, we shall look at some sociological approaches which do more than merely try to provide economic man with some flesh and blood.

Identity as an alternative

The notion of identity is frequently used in the social sciences, and it has also been used by economic sociologists who have studied markets (Miller, Jackson, Thrift, Holbrook, and Rowlands 1998; White 2008; Zuckerman 1999, 2000; Zuckerman, Kim, Ukanwa, and von Rittmann 2003). The notion has also been used by economists, but in a reductionist way, as the entire project seems to be to reduce identity to the traditional utility calculus (Akerlof and Kranton 2000, 2002, 2005, 2010), which means that preferences for all kinds of things are reduced to one and the same scale, utility, to enable rational calculation of the actors and modeling by the scientist. But in the version of Akerlof and Kranton, people's different identities may create utility. Their approach, nonetheless, builds a bridge of communication between economists and sociologists. This is a form of "friendly" economic imperialism, which essentially means to incorporate sociological ideas into the standard economic discourse.

We have seen that most economic sociologists start with the same atomistic approach as economics, and the attempt to correct the economic approach has essentially amounted to adding flesh and blood to economic man. The notion of identity at least acknowledges the social constitution of one identity by other identities. This is essentially what Harrison White (2002b, 2008) refers to, although it is possible to take the approach further and ground it in the socioontology of Martin Heidegger (2001a, 2001b). The consequence of this approach is that man's actions, by definition, are social, as Etzioni argues: "While it is possible to think abstractly about individuals apart from a community, if individuals were actually without community they would have very few of the attributes commonly associated with the notion of an individual person" (Etzioni 1988b: 202).[3]

What we propose is to provide a foundation for what has been called relational sociology (Emirbayer 1997). In contrast to economics and many economists who have followed the rational choice approach, Harrison White (1992, 2002b, 2008) has developed the idea of identity as an engine of change and as the pole of social order. It is this approach on which we shall build. It is, however, necessary to accept this argument for the other arguments presented in the book.

Identities are essentially relational, and their constitution is a social process, which is to say that identities cannot control themselves. In producer markets, to take one example, the consumers determine the identities of the producers (sellers). The actions of identities are to be understood in relation to their temporality, as attempts to obtain, keep, or change their identities. The question of whether action is social or not does not appear; the question is, instead, in which forms actions are social.

We define *identity* as a perceived similarity, bound by a narrative pegged to a "thing-event" (cf. Goffman 1968: 74–5). This is a generic definition of identity, which thus covers humans (e.g., Goffman 1968), organizations (Hatch and Schultz 2004), and things. This idea is not based on the idea that there is a world independent of us, which is simply endowed with meaning. The pegs are more deeply entrenched social constructs, which serve as pegs for less entrenched social constructs. Social constructs are meanings resulting from human activity and only human identities can bestow social identities on one another. Both individuals and collectives (such as firms) have reflexive capacity, famously noted by Keynes who talks about competitors thinking about what others think: "we devote our intelligence to anticipating what average opinion expects the average opinion to be" (Keynes 1973: 156). We may therefore speak of both individual and we-intentionality (Schmid 2005), referring to the fact that not only can an identity have an intention, but "we together," for example, the board of a company, may have intentions concerning what "we" do or want to do.

What we have presented so far, including the discussion of identity, may suggest that the market is mainly a structural system, and that actions are essentially consequences of markets. Structuralist network theory has had a strong impact on the sociology of markets, but it "falters when confronted with the fact that the same pattern of ties takes on different meanings and generates different effects, depending on the types of role relationship involved" (Phillips and Zuckerman 2001: 422). We argue that agency and identities are crucial, but that in existing markets they must be understood in relation to the market situation. We agree with Granovetter (1985, 1992) that action must be understood in relation to structure, but what we would also like to emphasize is that actors have cognitive capacities to reflect on their socially determined position and project acts to stay put or to try to change it.

To conceptualize agency in relation to identities is to acknowledge both the structural conditions of the social setting, and the intentionality of the actor. To accomplish this theoretically, we rely on levels of identity to handle both the structurally determined position of the actor, which we assume will affect her actions, but also her capacity to reflect on this position. Our action theory covers persons and organizations, for example, firms, and allows for gender to be treated, which is also the reason we have waited until now to make use of the female gender. We use identities rather than persons to capture the fact that persons behave differently when acting in a market, than with friends, or with their family, or firms operating in different markets. This is not to deny that one should understand a person or an organization as a whole, but only to assert that actors have different identities in different markets. Economic actors' identities have narratives in markets and explanations of their actions must account for this. A machine shop that sells the services of the combination of machines, lathes, and mills, faces buyers when they look in the direction of selling, and this renders the firms an identity; but it also gains identities as a buyer in the labor market and the markets for input material. This reflects the multiple identities of actors in different markets, which are embedded in each other.

Actors' identities are generated in different ways, depending on what type of market they operate in. An actor gains her identity in relation to other actors in the market with whom she shares a role, for example, traders on the stock exchange, or producers of cars. We call this identity collective, since the actor can affect it only indirectly; it is largely ascribed to her as a result of partaking in a market.

It is on the basis of this collective identity that is formed in the market that we refer to reflexive identity. By this we mean the reflexive capacity (Warde 1994) of both organizations and persons to perceive, think, plan, and act, given the situation in which they operate. Our point is that the actor has to take into account both what she wants to be in the market, and obviously the situation in the market – including her own identity in the market as seen by others – when acting. The tension between what she is and what she wants to be (reflexive identity) provides the potential scope for action.

The general point is that actors' track records in the market make up the narratives of their identities. Identity means coherence over time, and any calculation and any action of a single identity in a market must be understood in relation to its narrative. Although market actors share a cognitive structure of a market, they may have entered it with different interests. They have also gained identities in the market. The result is that the different identities will respond differently to what happens in markets. Interpretations – by human identities as well as by collective identities – are essential elements for action and dynamics, also in the economy.

Summary

This chapter has provided a short history of markets. To cover the entire literature on markets and to trace their history would be a huge task, beyond the scope of this book. We have shown, nonetheless, that markets need an institutional bedrock made up of basic trust, shared cognitive frameworks and rules if they are to function. The market appears to have grown out of gift, barter and trade. Equally, the market presupposes the trust that originally was found only in trading networks. The market, we may say, comes from networks (White 2002b). It should also be clear that markets are often the result of specific decisions and that the role of the deliberate organization of markets must be taken seriously. In chapter 7 we return to the question of how markets evolve, but before we do this, much more must be said about different forms of markets, since we may assume that not all market evolution follows the same path.

This chapter has not only discussed markets in terms of form, but also their contents, especially the underlying values and interests of market participants. This led us to an analysis of the assumptions of humanity that serve as the bedrock for market theories, and we outlined the difference between sociological and economic theories. We have seen that markets are not inherently correlated with rational capitalism. Markets, however, have gradually replaced other forms of coordination, and a liberal capitalism has gradually – and in a growing number of countries – become the cultural value that underpins and makes rationally planned actions in markets legitimate. The process of marketization has meant that we have seen more markets, also in areas of social life which previously were outside the economic realm. Finally, we looked at the role of man in market theories. It was shown that especially neoclassical economic theory has many of its implications rooted in assumptions of human beings. A sociological alternative, based on identity, was presented.

4

Forms of Markets

The purpose of this chapter is to discuss the various distinctions that have been drawn in the literature, but also to evaluate them. With the market definition provided in the first chapter, the relationship described to other forms of economic coordination, the overview of markets across time and space, and the analysis of the consequences of markets in society, we have presented a background to, and provided a number of tools for, analyzing markets. This chapter uses the theoretical notions introduced in chapter 1 to analyze markets further.

Our discussion of markets has so far been general, referring to all markets. Although it is obvious that not all markets are the same, many economists have continued to assume that there is one pure form, and that all others are simply deviations from the one presented by Walras. This form of market is also, for many, the ideal.

Despite the substantial contribution by anthropologists and sociologists to our understanding of markets, among sociologists only Harrison White has made a theoretical advance to the extent that one can talk of a market theory rigorous enough to challenge the neoclassical model of the market. White (in Swedberg 1990: 83) is clear about the fundamental differences between forms of market. He points out that economists only have a theory of exchange markets, in which already existing products are traded, while White has developed a theory of what he calls producer markets, in which the products somehow are connected to a production chain of markets. The neoclassical market will be discussed in chapter 5, and White's theory in chapter 6. The distinctions made in this chapter will also be used in the following chapters to see, for example, how questions of price and valuation are solved in different ways in different markets.

We begin by looking at the market elements that are included and implicit in the definition of the market, such as social structure and actors' interest. Then we turn to the prerequisites of markets: (1) what is traded; (2) the culture enframing how it is traded; and (3) how the things traded are valued. It is in light of the distinctions discussed in this chapter that we can begin to sort markets, and to understand in what ways they function differently. We will also look at market boundaries and market places.

Market Elements

We have defined a *market* as a social structure for the exchange of rights in which offers are evaluated and priced, and compete with one another. We will now look more closely at the elements of the definition to see how each of them affects the order of markets. To what extent can these elements explain observed market differences? We begin by looking at the social structure, followed by the different prerequisites introduced in chapter 1. The notion of property right, although essential, is not further problematized in this discussion.

Social structure

The market definition we have proposed has social structure as one of its core elements. At the most general level, social structure in markets is constituted by the roles of "buyer" and "seller." For a market to come into being there must be actors who can be identified as buyers or sellers. In a traditional bazaar, or in the local market for currency in the streets outside the bazaar in Istanbul, participants frequently switch between being buyers or sellers. They are more accurately described as traders of different

currencies. In other markets, firms and individuals develop identities or brands so that they constantly enact the role of seller.
The Coca Cola Company, to take one example, does not have to
inform us that it wants to be identified as the seller of Coke, as this
is well known. All of us are used to acting as consumers in different
markets, such as those for food, soft drinks, and garments.

This leads us to an important distinction, between markets in
which actors hold more or less permanent roles as either "buyer"
or "seller," and markets in which actors switch roles. Let us call
the first type "fixed-role markets," and the second "switch-role
markets." This is an ideal-typical distinction between two mutually exclusive market forms. The distinction, in other words,
separates markets in which actors' identities are tied to a more
general role that encompasses the two roles of buyer and seller
from those in which actors "permanently" take the role of either
buyer or seller.

The stock exchange, with its traders who switch roles between
"buyer" and "seller" several times a day, is the typical example of
a switch-role market. Swap markets, financial markets, and currency markets are additional examples of switch-role markets, in
which actors switch roles and appear on both sides of the market
interface. Also, markets for metals futures and other rights, which
can be exchanged many times before the contract is due to expire,
are examples of switch-role markets. Real estate agents may, in
some countries, act on behalf of customers as buyers and sometimes as sellers of properties. The market for emissions rights is yet
another example of switch-role markets.

The neoclassical market model refers to switch-role markets,
in which everyone is simply an atom capable of signing contracts
as buyer and seller. Economic man has no identity as "seller,"
"buyer," "producer," or "consumer." This idea of the market as
a social formation in which actors do not hold permanent roles
is merely a reflection of the fact that Walras developed his theory
by looking at the Paris stock exchange. This stock exchange,
like any other, is a place where "traders" sell and buy rights or,
more precisely, shares in companies or derivatives, that is, rights
to buy or sell a right at a given price in the future. The notion of

"trader" seems, etymologically, to refer to the course of action, namely, what one does. Trading is the activity associated with people in a trade who engage in economic transactions with one another and with people from other trades. An actor in a stock exchange market, for example, has an identity as trader, agent, and dealer, but not an identity as seller or buyer (C. Smith 1981). Trader is thus a more general role, which encompasses the roles of "buyer" and "seller." Their trading services, however, are offered on the fixed-role markets in which they are permanently identified as sellers. This is, thus, a producer market for trading services. Despite the accuracy of the neoclassical model as an account of the stock exchange, it is almost a paradox that the most influential theory of markets is not able to account properly for what goes on in most of the markets we observe. The majority of real markets – such as those for beer, cars, ships, or garments, and the market for traders' services – are fixed-role markets, in which the market identity of each actor is fixed (tied) to only one side of the market (producer/seller or consumer/buyer). Thus, car manufacturers (such as BMW, Ford, and Honda) have identities that are tied to the role of sellers (producers) of cars. The role of seller is fixed in the consumer market, which means that they do not also operate as consumers (buyers) of cars. This is not to deny that car manufacturers operate as buyers in labor markets or in markets for tires, organizational consultants, and many other inputs. Car producers are nonetheless identified as sellers in the market that generates their identity as car producers. This market, in other words, is the core market in the car industry, and the activities of actors in the industry are ultimately oriented to this market. This is illustrated in figure 4.1.

Although economic sociologists have rightly pointed out the centrality of producer markets, they have mainly discussed producers in markets and neglected consumers. We are accustomed to the role of consumer and often take part in markets, sometimes several times a day. In some markets we act frequently, such as food markets; in others, such as the market for new cars, less frequently. In many markets we are anonymous, in the sense that the producers do not know us as individuals, as when we buy a

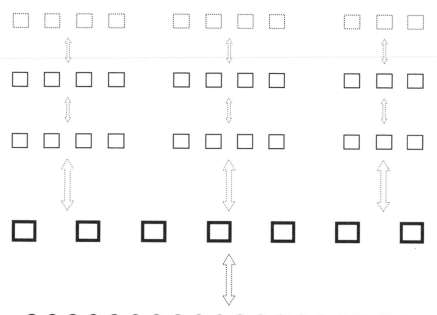

Figure 4.1 Interconnected markets in an industry, presented schematically. Each arrowhead represents a specific market. Boxes with thick lines are core producers and the circles represent final consumers. Boxes with thin lines are producers of different inputs. The core producers are buyers in three markets. Each of the producers in these three markets is operating as a buyer in yet other markets.

pair of sneakers at the mall. We may in other markets know the sellers, for example, at our favorite bar. In the eyes of producers, final consumers are usually only "known" as ideal-types. That is to say that we as individuals "represent" a category, such as "demanding," "price conscious," or "fashion-oriented" customers. This categorization and differentiation of customers is carried out by firms that may face millions of customers in their stores. Also, consumers differentiate among themselves in terms of different categories. In business-to-business markets, firms may know of each other, not least since these markets usually have fewer actors, but also since, at least in some of them, each deal is relatively more important than single deals in a final consumer market.

Although sociologists have played down the role of the consumer, they have, in contrast to economists, realized that most markets in fact are fixed-role markets. Consequently, most studies are of various types of producer markets, which are characterized by an array of producers identified as sellers. The sociological literature usually draws on the works of Harrison White (e.g., 1981, 2002b). White credits Edward Chamberlin, and to some extent also Alfred Marshall, for initiating this stream of thought that acknowledges how markets function. Moreover, in producer markets, such as White's example of the market for frozen pizza, producers normally offer slightly different products. This is not a necessary condition of a fixed-role market, as when different construction consortia compete for a contract to build a bridge. In this case the sellers (producers) offer the same product, the construction of a bridge according to the specifications of the buyers, but at different prices.

The crucial notions for understanding the distinction between switch-role and fixed-role markets are, hence, identity and role, not the goods and their purported essential characteristics. Actors in switch-role markets are not identified with any side of the market, as is the case in a fixed-role market. But another feature of switch-role markets, characterized by incumbents who cannot be identified as either buyer or seller, is that the social structure is made up of the two roles of seller and buyer. The difference, to reformulate what we have just said, is that in this sort of market, actors are identified with the more general notion of market actor, such as broker or trader.

Interest, role and market form

The full importance of this distinction between markets in which actors switch roles and those in which they identify themselves, and are identified by others, with one side of the market, will only be seen in the next chapter. But it is clear from a sociological point of view that the market struggle already mentioned by Weber as a defining characteristic of the market is affected by how the market is ordered. This relationship between market structure and interest was clearly noted by Geertz, who says that the bazaar, which we define as a switch-role market, is characterized by competition between "buyer and seller" and not, "as it is for most of the firm economy," between "seller and seller" (Geertz 1963: 33). Struggle, as mentioned above, has to do with conflicting interests (Swedberg 2003, 2004).

Those who are identified with one side are likely to join together to push their common interests, and perhaps even organize the market (Geertz 1963: 29). The identification with one side of the market, for example, buyers, and its interests, does not mean that we deny rivalry between buyers. But the common interest is a condition for them to join hands and strengthen their position vis-à-vis the sellers, for example, by determining the conditions of trade. An organization which has other organizations as members – the buyers in a market, to take one example – may thus facilitate the organized interest activities of the buyers' side, as was shown in the example of American shoemakers (Commons 1909).

In switch-role markets, actors do not have interests as sellers or buyers, as they are not identified with one side of the market, but as market actors. We can presume that this facilitates cooperation among market actors, as all share an interest in a well-functioning market which provides opportunities for profit. There is, in other words, no long-term conflict between market roles. Although actors, such as brokers, may compete in the market for market share, there can be no organized interest among "sellers" or "buyers" as all participants represent both, or neither, of the two sides. There is, however, strong common interest among the traders to maintain trading, since this is what generates their revenue, regardless of the trend of the market. This is a reason for actors to create markets.

Switch-role markets may also be more difficult to understand, since the roles and the interests are less clearly visible. We should, therefore, not be surprised that people who are in the market, but who do not line up on one side, as actors do in producer markets, talk of "the market" in a more mystical way. A few citations will show what I mean. Charles Smith, who not only has been in the market, but has also studied it in great detail, reports one informant saying: "The only thing that is clear about the market is that nothing is clear" (Smith 1981: 11). In a similar fashion, Hassoun reports how market actors regard it as something that is "alive," saying, for example, that "'the market is jumpy'" or "'It was healthier' [today]" (Hassoun 2005: 109). Charles Smith alludes to the market as "mindless" (Smith 1981: 142), opting for an explanation that we can trace back to Pareto, namely, that there are many different actors pursuing different strategies in a market. To this, we may add the reports on "the market" and its sentiments in the daily press. On this approach, the stock exchange is a game, in which you win and lose, and the winner on the day is the one who made the most money.

The Central Ordering Principles

It is clear that, although all markets are made up of buyers and sellers, and each market participant has its own interest – to get a high price (seller) or to get a low price (buyer) – one should acknowledge the phenomenologies of different market forms and the corresponding principles of order.

We have seen that looking at the social structure alone is not enough if we want to understand order. The distinction between switch-role and fixed-role markets is one of importance, but neither the only one nor necessarily the most important. What, then, is the key distinction to be used when analyzing market order? To account for order in different markets we must introduce the distinction that separates markets ordered by status from those ordered by standards. This distinction, too, is ideal-typical, and refers to two mutually exclusive categories. In a "status" market, order is maintained because the identities of actors on both sides of the market are ranked according to status, which is a more entrenched social construction than the standard of the offer (commodity or service) traded in the market. However, if the sets of buyers' and sellers' identities are more entrenched than the offers, we speak of a status market. Such a set of sellers could be, for example, the different brands of jeans that compete with each other in a certain segment. In a market characterized by "standards," the situation is reversed: the offer is a more entrenched social construction than the identity rankings of actors in the market. There is a tipping point between status and standard in real markets, in the sense that one is always dominant. Markets in which the standard of the offers – more generally represented by the price-quality-delivery combination – are relatively more entrenched, or taken for granted, than the order of the social structure (such as the set of producers and/or the set of consumers) are standard markets. Examples are easy to find, such as where we have material categories rooted in unambiguous and stable material conditions, such as metal, cotton, and grain, although all of these, of course, also have to be turned into categories. Most existing markets are a mix of the two ideal-types, status and standard. Silver cutlery exemplifies this, the material preserves the economic worth of the material – since it can be sold for its worth in weight – but depending on design, the economic value differs for items of the same silver quality and weight.

Given these two distinctions, it is possible to separate markets into four categories. Table 4.1 presents these distinctions, including empirical examples of markets of each kind. Let us elaborate

Table 4.1 Market typology.
Empirical examples given the two distinctions between fixed-role and switch-role markets, and status and standard markets.

Typology of markets	*Fixed roles*	*Switch roles*
Standard	Wholesale market for flowers	Stock exchange
Status	Consumer market for garments	Bazaar

on each of these empirical examples. Flowers in wholesale markets are standardized items. This is not to say that all flowers sold are identical, but each sort of flower is traded separately, and it is normally not a problem to separate the different sorts from each other. There is, in addition, a quality scale, so that it is possible to speak of quality independently of price. Those who grow flowers sell them either directly on the market, or to an agent who then sells them in the market. Sellers, or producers, of flowers do not operate as buyers of flowers. In this case each market actor's identity is fixed to one role, either as buyer or as seller, and the ordering principle is the standard of the offer. The offer is not merely the product, in this case a batch of flowers, though this is clearly its base, but also how it is delivered. This means that actors, both sellers and buyers, can relate the offers, "a batch of flowers of a certain quality for a given price," independently of the transaction partner. The orientation, in other words, is to the offer and the standard, and only indirectly to trading partners. This is very similar to what has been observed by Garcia-Parpet (2007) regarding how the strawberry market she studied is organized.

In the stock exchange, the product is doubtless a standard, and this will be further studied in chapter 5. Any share of a company, such as General Motors, is identical to another share. This means that it does not matter at all who is the buyer or the seller. As a consequence, the market depends less on who is there, and the price of the offers (stocks) becomes the ordering principle. This means that one can speak of order due to standardized offers to which actors orient themselves. The important point is whether there is a standard that is independent of the product so that the "quality" of the product can be measured. A special case of standard is when all products are identical, which is the case in stock markets. The market category or, more generally, the standard of the market, can be determined in the market, by the state or by market participants themselves, or one side thereof.

In the final consumer market for garments, where we act as consumers and firms with identities offer clothes, the product, subject to the vagaries of fashion, is everything but a standard. In a market ordered by status, the offers change, and there is no standard to evaluate what is offered that is independent of those who trade in the market. It is instead the social structure that is relatively stable, because the sellers, all of which advertise, have stores, and have usually been around for many years. That is to say that they have identities in relation to each other, and these identities are known by consumers. The important point is that some sellers have more status than others, and what they offer, and what high-status consumers purchase, determines what becomes fashionable. Fashion is "made" or "performed" as a result of interactions between producers and consumers, and not evaluated according to a given standard. There is no standard of fashion. In fact, all markets in which decisions boil down to aesthetic values lack a standard. These can be seen as aesthetic markets (Aspers 2001: 1; Entwistle 2009), a notion that represents a certain part of status markets, in which decisions are based on aesthetic values or, in other words, taste (Bourdieu 1984).

Sellers of garments, for example, The Gap, Zara, and H&M, are relatively few, and consumers can keep track of their identities. Consumers are of course not known as individuals by the sellers of garments, nor do they know each other. What both sellers and buyers know are ideal-typical consumers, such as upper-class people with their take on fashion, people in the art world, and all manner of sub-groups. This social structure is not eternal, but it is more stable – and can therefore be a stronger principle of order – than the offers in the market.

The final example is the classical bazaar. The bazaar is made up of traders who buy and sell. The bazaar is not concentrated on one item; instead, "everything" may be found in the market, although bazaars like those in Istanbul are divided – often spatially – into sections for food or garments and, within those where food is sold, you find the fish traders concentrated in one place and those who trade in meat and so on, concentrated in another. Today, many bazaars have gradually been transformed into market places in which sellers offer goods to final consumers, but this has not always been the case. Clifford Geertz, for example, says that "Commodities . . . once injected into the market network tend to move in circles, passing from trader to trader for a fairly extended period before they come within the reach of a genuine consumer" (1963: 31). Having discussed the market elements, such as the social structure of actors with interests that result in competition, and property rights, we will turn to the three prerequisites for an ordered market, discussed above, that will have to be met in any market, though in different forms.

1. What the market is about

In a standard market, such as the market for copper, it is clear what is on offer. Even in markets ordered by status, such as the art markets described by Velthuis (2005) or Plattner (1996), it is reasonably clear what is traded and what is not traded. In this case offers are traded. An offer can be a material object, such as cutlery or a basketball, or it can be a service, such as tax consultancy. The offer may be open to negotiations, but not everything can be open for interpretation and negotiation. Some sort of stability is created by the fact that a market is characterized by what is traded. If the objects or services of trade are stable, it is easy to understand that market actors can orient themselves to this, and that it is clear about what the market is. In fashion markets, as we have just established, change is the key. However, this is clear to the participants in the market. It is this cognitive similarity and shared frame (Goffman 1974) of the market and what is traded in the market – even if it is about change – that matters. Thus, markets are partly separated due to the perception of the categories traded (Rosa, Porac, Runser-Spanjol, and Saxon 1999) by consumers and producers, which is why we can talk of a "market category" (Kennedy 2005). We do not need to focus on the psychological-cognitive dimension of categories; it is the social process of their construction and existence that is of key importance. Hence, markets presuppose the singularization of the offers traded in order to make them calculable (Callon and Muniesa 2005). Each market, in other words, values one thing (Favereau, Biencourt, and Eymard-Duvernay 2002).

The world does not come ready-made with market categories. These have to be made. Some of these categories can be made outside the market place, and then included in a market. Other categories may be traded, but not yet in a market, and yet others have to be made by market actors themselves. The market actors may produce the market categories in a spontaneous process, but they may also be the result of attempts to organize categories (cf. Möllering 2009). Standardization (cf. Brunsson et al. 2000) is one way in which categories are made as a result of organization. It may not be so hard to imagine that steel, which is a man-made product, has been subject to standardization. But even more natural objects, such as fish (Holm 2008) and timber, are divided into categories. Timber is divided into timber for mills and timber for pulp, as well as timber to be used for heating and other purposes. But also within the category of timber, there is much variation. There are different trees, such as pine and birch and spruce, but there are, in addition, timber qualities for each sort of tree.

We can conclude that each market is about something, and this something is usually what gives the market a name, such as the market for human organs (Healy 2006), which are not sold in the same market as cars. In other words, "things" which in one sense are similar are traded in the "same" market. A central sociological point is that these things cannot be reduced to material conditions.

2. How things are done in the market

The second prerequisite has to do with culture in the market. We define *culture* as beliefs, norms, "tools," and behaviors – for example, discourse and practice – appropriate to the setting. Culture refers to both informal institutions, out of which formal institutions, such as rules and laws, grow. There are cultural elements that constitute the background for all social interactions, and those that are similar to many markets and others that are unique to a specific market. Market culture may thus be divided into general traits that separate it from non-markets, but also traits that make particular markets unique and separate them from other markets; the latter can be called partial (market) culture. Although culture itself cannot be the result of decision-making, often rules and institutions are decided upon. The overall notion of culture encompasses decided and grown elements, and it cannot be determined a priori which sort is the most important in a market.

We begin with general market culture. As markets become part of the lifeworld of most contemporary "market societies" (Slater and Tonkiss 2001), it is possible to identify a general market culture that spans many markets and that can be called into action when people act and when markets are made. Thus, market actors can use a repertoire of toolkits (Swidler 1986) in order to act, which are legitimate in many different markets. The culture of a market helps to bring it in order, as it prescribes what can, and cannot, be done, and its corresponding sanctions. The legal principle of merchants, the so-called *lex mercatoria*, is one example of a formal institution that regulates behavior in markets (Volckart and Mangels 1999). Culture in the second sense – that is, general market prerequisites – is valid in many markets and such prerequisites are important for the constitution of markets. The general market culture also refers to what is "worthy": "Worthy objects are *salable* goods that have a *strong position* in the market. Worthy persons are rich, *millionaires*, and they *live the high life*" (Boltanski and Thévenot 2006: 196).

What do we mean by the partial culture of a specific market or, for short, the specific market culture? A market may, to various degrees, have a unique "culture" which can be manifested in its narrative (Mützel 2007), which actors who operate in it acquire in processes of socialization. Thus, not only does culture order a market, but it may also constitute it as a unique market. This refers to such simple matters as who contacts whom (who makes offers: the seller or the buyer); who pays for lunch; and many more things that are the result of custom. Furthermore, the culture of a specific market covers the idea of "rules of exchange" (Fligstein and Mara-Drita 1996: 15; Smith 2007: 3; White 2002b: 2), in short, how market actors are allowed and expected to cooperate and compete in the market. Cultural aspects can include how people talk, what an office should look like, or – for successful fashion photographers, for example – what kind of car they should be driving (Aspers 2006: 52–3). Scripts for price-setting – that is, how to get the output price for oil paintings (Velthuis 2005) or any other items – also differ between markets. How economic value is decided will be discussed in the next section.

Culture in the last two senses – the general and the partial culture of a specific market – in combination, could potentially order a market, as both concern rules of conduct that enable, facilitate, and restrain human coordination. Although culture is an essential component in all markets and a condition of any social interaction, it is less common for culture to be the most entrenched ordering principle in markets. Nonetheless, in some markets, culture may be of great importance, especially when we talk of market places. A market place is not necessarily associated with a single commodity, and hence not a specific social structure of known buyers and sellers. What we find is usually, as in the case of the bazaar, traders who populate the market place waiting for the consumers to come and be caught in their net. Although each product may be said to have its own market, neither of these is strong enough to order the market place. It is rather the market place that orders the different "markets." Geertz has studied markets with low formal organization, which is to say that guilds and formal supervision are missing. Instead, order must largely be seen as a result of "fixed customs of trade hallowed by centuries of continuous use" (Geertz 1963: 47). Lisa Bernstein has studied the diamond trade, finding a trade with markets that has set up its own rules, all of which are embedded in social networks and tacitly assumed codes. She says, to take one example, that "the sophisticated traders who dominate the industry have developed an elaborate, internal set of rules, complete with distinctive institutions and sanctions, to handle disputes among industry members" (Bernstein 1992: 115).

3. Determining the economic worth of the offer

The third prerequisite that must be met is the determination of economic (exchange) value. The other two prerequisites are specific to markets, but the value of goods must also be determined in organizations that have to deal with the questions of production, consumption, and distribution. The economic value of luxurious goods, such as champagne and caviar, was not the result of market "decisions" in Russia during the Soviet era. It was instead a political decision about how much champagne and caviar should be produced and what they should cost (Gronow 2003). A consequence of the politically decided prices in the Soviet Union was that caviar and champagne were cheap, which meant that people valued these goods less.

We have already explained that an object to be traded in a market must be seen as legitimate, which reflects "moral" values in society. The third prerequisite refers to how worth in *economic* terms is determined. Value is inherent in the process of comparison, which is a condition of competition that we have argued is an essential element of markets. There are thus different ways of generating market value. The conflict of interest of trading parties can be resolved in processes of haggling, bargaining, by fixed prices, or with the help of an auction. These are thus forms of exchanging goods, which over time have existed depending on values of cultural, moral, or economic nature.

The normal way of determining value in fixed-role markets is to offer goods or services at fixed prices. In this case, price-setting is identical to the determination of market value, provided that there are buyers willing to meet the offers and that there is competition. Some actors may be willing to pay more to get the object, or sell it at a lower price than the price in the market, creating added value to these people. In producer markets where products differ, such as the market for bicycles, there is essentially a price at which each different kind of bicycle is offered. Although there may be some room for price negotiation between the customer and the dealer (and between the dealer and the manufacturer or wholesaler), the price is essentially of a "take it or leave it" character for the customer. This we also see when we are looking at the prices of different detergent brands in the supermarket. The buying of military aircraft, in contrast, may take years and involve all kinds of negotiations, sometimes at the highest political level.

However, fixed prices, in the sense that we find prices quoted in advertisements, in stores, in restaurants and elsewhere, have not always been the norm. The bazaar is one example of a trading place where we do not find prices. This has historical reasons, as Geertz explains, in modern economic terms:

> The sliding price system, accompanied by the colorful and often aggressive bargaining which seems to mark such systems everywhere, is in part simply a means of communicating economic information in an indeterminate pricing situation ... [and it] is to a degree a mere reflex of the fact that the absence of complex bookkeeping and long-run costs or budgetary accounting makes it difficult for either the buyer or the seller to calculate very exactly what, in any particular case, a "reasonable" price is. (Geertz 1963: 32–3)

In situations in which historical pricing records are missing, the skills of those participating in the sometimes time-consuming process become important. Haggling involves parties making offers and counter-offers, and struggling over the price. In the bazaar there is thus a certain form of struggle, primarily between sellers and buyers, but also between sellers competing for customers. Also in a producer market, such as the market for washing machines, the struggle and the competition are among the sellers; as a buyer you can be pretty certain that there will be machines for sale on the market.

What is price? The monetary price, according to the economic view, is identical to its market price. Economic market value, in practical terms, is equivalent to the transaction price, that is, the price a buyer pays and the seller gets, not including possible transaction costs. Economists, moreover, see the market as a mechanism that generates prices. Stigler says, "The market is the area within which price is determined: the market is that set of suppliers and demanders whose trading establishes the price of a good" (Stigler and Sherwin 1985: 555). This means that price, in economics, is the result of market interaction.

But it is clear that both Stigler and Geertz refer only to an auction market. In status markets, to illustrate one difference, price is part of what constitutes the identity of the participants in the market. At least some status markets share one aspect of the markets that Veblen described, namely, that the demand for certain goods increases when the price goes up and the status of the producers may rise as a function of the price of the goods (Veblen 1953). This, to recall, is possible only because there is no scale of value that can be used to measure the "quality" of the goods, independently of those who buy and sell these goods.

Economic value is usually expressed in prices and quoted in monetary terms. Prices imply that products can be compared with other commodities and services. Prices, expressed in one form of money or another (cf. "money of account," Dodd 2005), enable us to compare completely different things, such as a car with a trip to Hawaii, but also two cars in the same market.

Prices can be set in different ways, since markets are different. In most switch-role markets, different kinds of auctions are used for setting prices. Auctions are perhaps the most common theoretical representation of price-setting, although empirically it is not the most common. There are different sorts of auctions (Smith 1989). The most common is the so-called English auction, which normally has a starting bid, from which the price is expected to ascend when bidders start to compete. A normal art auction, be it at Sotheby's or on the Internet (eBay), is organized as an English auction. The winning bid – that is, the price for which a good is exchanged for money – is equivalent to the market price. A so-called "Dutch auction" can be seen as an English auction but going in the opposite direction. It starts with a high price and is reduced until a buyer can be found. This is potentially a very fast form of auction, as those who organize the auction can reduce the prices rapidly, but it also calls for buyers who can make decisions quickly. The Dutch auction is used mostly for professionals, for example, when flowers are sold in Holland (figure 4.2), but also by the Ontario Flower Growers Co-operative, an organization set up in 1972. The Dutch auction allows several lots to be sold at once, which means that large quantities can be traded quickly.

In real life, we find auctions in all kinds of combinations, also for the same kinds of object. The organization of fish markets, to take one example, varies, and in Iceland there are

thirty two auctions, eighteen of which are English ("rising price") and fourteen of which are Dutch ("descending price"). At Lorient

Figure 4.2 Aalsmeer flower auction, with descending prices.

Source: Druifkes, Wikimedia Commons

in France, fish is sold through a combination of pairwise trading and auction, while at Sète it is sold by Dutch auction, and at nearby Marseille by pairwise trading. The fish market in Sydney, Australia, is conducted as two simultaneous Dutch auctions. (Kirman 1991: 157)

Auctions are discussed in the literature, especially by economists (Krishna 2009), but also by sociologists (Smith 1989). The US Treasury and other governments use auctions as a means of borrowing money from the market at the lowest cost possible. The word itself – auction – is of Latin origin and means "to increase" (Krishna 2009: 2). Auctions, when several bidders are involved, will generate a price that at least reaches above what the buyer with the second highest bid offered.

Auctions may be "open," so that all prices are public. Open – at least to the participants – auctions are the most common form. In other cases, buyers are asked to submit sealed bids, from which the seller chooses. The first (highest) bid may also be the winning bid. There is also the sealed-bid, second-price auction, in which the highest bidder wins the auction, but pays not the amount of his bid, but that of the second highest bid. In some Swedish counties, forest land is sold by sealed-bid auction (with no starting price), but in a neighboring county there may be a starting "accept price," although if it is expected that several buyers will show an interest in the property by filling out a form, there will be an English auction to decide the winning bid. This wide variation suggests that we must understand the organization of a market in a historical light, and that it cannot be reduced to a universal principle of rationality.

A market exists only when we know what is traded, the culture of the market, and if there is a way of setting price, that is, when the market prerequisites have been met; only then can comparison and competition come about. With this insight, we turn to the question of the boundaries of markets – more specifically, to what extent can the market elements, including the three prerequisites, be used for understanding the boundaries between markets?

Market Boundaries

This book is called *Markets*, not "the market" or "the market society." The reason is that we want to draw distinctions between different forms of markets, but of course also between empirical markets. To distinguish between markets, we must look at the boundaries of markets. When does a market begin, and when does it end? We begin by providing more reasons why the issue of market boundaries is important, and then apply our tools to the different sorts of markets we can observe.

To define markets and to draw lines between markets is not merely of theoretical interest. Understanding market boundaries is a condition of defining market shares. It is simple to find out what a company's market share is: you only have to divide its revenues by the revenues of the market as a whole. But "Calculations of market share or market concentration, terms typically used to assess conditions of competition, have little meaning if the boundaries of the market have not been correctly defined" (Brooks 1995: 536). The problem, thus, is to define what firms and what products are included in a market. In the field of cell-phones, Nokia has for many years been the leading producer, with a market share of almost 50 percent. Reality is more complex, however, and markets – and market boundaries – may not be stable. When Apple and other suppliers came in from other markets, offering customers a technological alternative to the traditional cell-phones offered by Siemens, Ericsson, and Nokia, the market was redefined. In this case, it is unclear what the market is about and what the boundaries – that is, the environment – of different markets are. Hence, real market boundaries are often ambiguous to define. States, such as the US government, and its Department of Justice and the Federal Trade Commission, have to evaluate mergers and acquisitions in terms of whether companies will thereby gain a monopoly position, enabling them to raise prices and thus hinder competition, increasing their profits at the expense of consumers.[1]

Many economists have tried to define market boundaries based on the idea of standard or, as economists say, homogeneous products. This means that markets are defined based on the offers traded. A correlated idea is that prices are identical in markets. Stigler uses this approach by connecting price and market: "The central role of price in defining a market is the reciprocal side of this relationship between price determination and market determination" (Stigler and Sherwin 1985: 555). The argument is that if a price difference can be observed between two places in which the same product is offered, there are two different markets. The market, they argue, should be understood as "the area within which price is determined: the market is that set of suppliers and demanders whose trading establishes the price of a good" (Stigler and Sherwin 1985: 555). This attempt to define the market and its boundaries is based on the idea of the perfect market with a standardized supply, which results in an equilibrium. This definition also implies that any form of product differentiation, such as the flavor of chewing gums, represents market differentiation. This conclusion would not be accepted by many people in light of the competitive pressure in any market in which branding is important.

How, then, have sociologists tried to define market boundaries? The first condition, of course, is that there is competition between those in the market. If we follow our distinction between status and standard market, one strategy comes to mind. The border of a standard market is determined by those who make competitive offers of the standardized product. If there is a scale, only products with a certain "quality range," for example, potatoes of a certain required standard, may potentially be in that market. This indicates also the value of the economic approach. In a status market, in contrast, we should not seek the border of the market "in" the goods, but "in" the social structure. It is then the relations between the actors in the market that matters, but only between producers; to understand this, we must also account for the consumers. The sociological approach, which we have presented, starts with the idea of order, not equilibrium.

The sociologists Ronald Burt and Debbie Carlton (1989) have analyzed the boundaries for fixed-role markets, referring to "producers" and "consumers", defined in terms of their transaction networks. Could their analysis be extended to include interaction patterns among traders in a switch-role market, such as the market for foreign currency or a traditional stock exchange? We may expect that the interaction pattern between traders in stock exchanges, in which identical offers (goods) are traded, will not show signs of networks, or of transaction and information transmission. But it is exactly this that Wayne Baker (1984) found in an empirical study of the floor trading of stock options. Today, with automatic trading, this is less likely. Nonetheless, social bonding, to make sure that information possessed by one actor is not made public as soon as it is shared with a trusted partner in the industry, is still important. This, however, is done largely outside the market, in clubs and pubs (Hasselström 2003). What we tend to see is only a shift in the network structure, which previously could be observed in the market, to less observable, even hidden, networks (Simmel 1955).

However, although Burt and Carlton provide evidence of interaction patterns which facilitates a discussion of market boundaries, they cannot separate markets ordered by status from those ordered by standard, as the "commodity" is already assumed. They are, nonetheless, explicit about the cause of market boundaries: "Markets are bounded as network phenomena by differences between patterns of buying and selling imposed by production technologies" (Burt and Carlton 1989: 724).

To understand why we observe a certain network pattern of a market, we must investigate the causes of the boundaries and look at the form of market. Stock markets are not different because of "production technologies" or different trading technologies. In everyday language, we often refer to the boundaries in relation to what is traded, such as the market for tractors or the market for shampoo. Products are in many cases the most entrenched social construction of the market, so that we can talk of standard markets. In these cases the product is standardized enough not only to gain the name of the product, but also to define the market's borders. The strawberry market studied by Marie-France Garcia-Parpet (2007) is a clear example of a market in which the product – strawberries – is entrenched. Apples and peaches are traded in other markets. A standard or, in terms of the prerequisites, what the market is about, is one way of separating one market from another. However, when the same sort of cars are sold in several different countries, is this not one market? No, although the standards – if this applies at all to car markets – can be identical in different countries, there are other things that separate them. From the perspective of network analysis, it is clear that we should define a market and its boundaries in terms of relations. According to Burt and Carlton, "[t]o the extent that producers of one commodity and producers of another have identical relations with the same supplier markets and identical relations to the same consumer markets, they are competitors in the same production market" (Burt and Carlton 1989: 724). From a network perspective, these relations are structurally equivalent, and this is the decisive reason why the firms are in the same market. This leaves out the content, but the advantage gained is a view of the relations, and thus the structure, instead of focusing on the products.

This finding indicates the relevance of network analysis, but is not necessarily either a cause or an effect of the boundaries we observe. We cannot on any logical grounds (Quine 1961) give the network perspective explanatory primacy, that is, grant one approach the role of the true or first explanation, in relation to which others are only auxiliary explanations. This pattern can be observed because of cultural reasons, which can be concretized in terms of either formal (legal) or informal institutional reasons. Government or self-regulated licensing that restricts the number of market actors may also be the reason for market boundaries. Theoretically, the same commodities may be sold in several markets although essentially the same actors take part in them, the only difference being that the markets are located in different places and the rules of engagement are different.

Market boundaries may be more or less flexible. Standard markets are easier to expand than status markets. In fact, most global markets, in the sense we have defined markets, deal with fairly standardized products. Let us take the markets for different currencies as one instance studied by, for example, Karin Knorr Cetina. Let us say, first, that these markets are inherently interconnected. You cannot, so to speak, buy US dollars with US dollars. You also have to sell a currency. In this way we talk of the exchange of currencies, so that you may buy US dollars with your euros, which is what currency markets are all about. Although you may go to a bank, foreign exchange outlet, or even Thomas Cook, to exchange currencies, most trading is done by traders sitting in front of screens. This is indeed a global market, and traders all over the world are connected. This is not to say there is free entry or that the traders are evenly distributed. In fact, London, New York, Tokyo, and Zürich are the main trading hubs, which together ensure that trading is a round-the-clock activity. It is a global market because exactly the same currencies are traded, which means that the first prerequisite of a market is met. They trade formal rights, since no physical money is moved, in contrast to the old metal currencies that traders used in European fairs in the twelfth century. The rules of the game are not determined locally; the game is instead formed in relation to the *lex mercatoria* principle (Knorr Cetina 2005: 57), suggesting that at least one important part of the second prerequisite is met at a global level. The same principle of price-setting is also in place, which means that the third prerequisite is also met. The spatial difference matters less as the interface is mainly, if not entirely, a matter of computer screens (Knorr Cetina and Bruegger 2002). Spatiality still matters on the micro scale, however, as a way of organizing knowledge among traders. This means that groups with similar skills can communicate, but also that they can inform other groups as well as take in new information. Finally, the third market prerequisite is also met, since the same way of determining the economic value of the different currencies is used in these large markets. We may also speak of local markets, such as the currency markets – some of which are illegal – in various countries where euros or dollars replace the official currency.

Organizing market boundaries

Market boundaries can be created by regulation. When the state decides to give one firm a monopoly position, this "closes" (Swedberg 1998; Weber 1978) that side of the market. Market boundaries can be due to organizational decisions, also outside the state. Haute couture is a form of fashion that is essentially organizational, and not primarily about the essence of clothes. The organization La Chambre Syndicale de la Couture Parisienne organizes fashion houses, and is a form of modern guild that has strict membership requirements, such as the number of designers employed and the number of garments made per day. The Chambre is a meta-organization that creates and controls market entry. It is primarily because of this organizational ordering that haute couture is different from prêt-à-porter ("ready-to-wear"), which refers to designer labels that produce for a larger group of consumers and with mass-production techniques, so that prices are lower (Kawamura 2004: 73–88). There are, of course, differences in how the garments for these markets are made, but the point is that this is not what sets them apart.

More fundamentally, the explanation of market boundaries must account for the phenomenology of the market in question. In other words, only if actors perceive it as a market can one really speak of a market; in those cases, we are also likely to identify the interaction pattern that Burt claims to be crucial. This is to take Harrison White's market approach seriously. White says that "Markets are tangible cliques of producers observing each other" (1981: 543). In this case, the market boundary becomes a corollary of the market.

In status markets, the products are not the reason for market boundaries. If we take a look at fashion garment markets, we see – simply by strolling along the main street in a large city every second week – that the products change. This suggests that there is no inherent "product quality" that can explain the market boundaries. What we find are sets of producers coming together and competing against each other. The activities of producers must be understood, however, in relation to consumer groups (Aspers 2010). The market boundary in a status market should be explained in terms of the perception of producers, who define their competitors and customers. This cannot be studied adequately by means of a network approach. Competitive relations, as well as direction of meaning flow in markets (such as when fashion is diffused by means of imitation), may not leave any "traces" or ties as there is no interaction, although we certainly have relations.

We can conclude the discussion on market boundaries by saying that the reasons for market boundaries cannot be known a priori. It must be understood first of all in relation to the form of market – status and standard – and in relation to the combined effect of the elements and prerequisites of markets. A market boundary can thus be rooted either in the social structure or in the standard. But an empirical market may have geographical boundaries; the market for restaurants is local, and there is no national competition, unless we look at the level of fast-food chains. Furthermore, culturally different markets may exist, as when different stock exchanges compete with one another. We will return to the issue of market category next, when we explain the distinction between market and market place.

Markets and Market Place

The notion of "market" refers, in historical and contemporary research, as well as in everyday language, both to the market process and to specific places. We will now clarify these different but often related ideas. By place, we are not referring simply to the fact that market actors are positioned in the same location. As we have seen, Karin Knorr Cetina and Urs Bruegger's (2002) study of the highly global currency market is best described as a virtual market; the participants watch each other on the screen, and orient themselves to this virtual market. By *market place*, we mean the socio-material infrastructure located in space that makes possible market transactions. A space has boundaries in relation to the environment (other spaces), and the boundaries may be geographical, such as the square in the middle of the town allotted to market transactions, or determined by membership, as in the global currency markets.

A market place may be used for, and refer to, one specific market, or to several different markets. By this means, individual markets and also single transactions, some of which may constitute a prelude to a market, can take place. In other words, the market place today is the modern version of the trading place of the city, which we saw emerging when we discussed markets in history. Today, market actors may not fear death or robbery, but remedies for uncertainty, efficiency, and competition are still needed. One may say that the place provides actors who have a specific interest with an infrastructure, which may be composed of technical devices for trading, but also rules and supervision, for the determination of what is traded and how to trade and behave in the market. A trader, however, can be physically located almost anywhere in the world. The highly organized stock exchange, to which we will return in the next chapter, is a good example of a market place that facilitates the trade of different stocks, each essentially being a market on its own. This infrastructure is there to be used, even though a single actor operates infrequently in any of its specific markets. Next we will look at a particular form of market place, namely, the bazaar.

The bazaar

The bazaar is an ancient institution, probably with Persian roots. It is a market place, what many would call a market, or simply the "daily market." It is a physical place, which is directed to final consumers; the word "bazaar" literally means "strolling back and forth," and the European version – arcades – inspired Walter Benjamin to reflect on modern society (2002). People stroll in narrow streets, sometimes covered by a roof, and small shops are located side by side. This form of marketing, and market place, was imported to Europe in the seventeenth century. The idea of a bazaar economy, as used here, is, however, wider and covers both the form of organizing business as well as how transactions are carried out. Although our focus is on the bazaar as a market place, it is good to take a closer look at it empirically, before returning to the theoretical explanation of this type of market. We will follow Clifford Geertz's work on bazaars, based on his studies in the 1950s in Indonesia. Of course, other sources could be used.

The first thing we should note is that the bazaar cannot be separated from the rest of society; it is, as Geertz puts it, "imbedded" (Geertz 1963: 32). Although contemporary society is differentiated into several spheres of life, there is no way one can treat economic actions as completely separate, and this is indeed the case with the economies Geertz studied. In the following, he refers to a particular market place in Modjukuto, Indonesia:

> Thus by the *pasar* [the market] we mean not simply that particular square eighth of a mile or so of sheds and platforms, set apart in the center of the town, where (as someone has said of the classical emporium) men are permitted each day to deceive one another, but the whole pattern of small-scale peddling and processing activity characteristic of the Modjukuto area generally. The market place is the climax of this pattern, its focus and center, but it is not the whole of it;

for the *pasar* style of trading permeates the whole region, thinning out somewhat in the most rural of villages. (Geertz 1963: 30)

We have already mentioned that the bazaar is one form of economic transaction that we should look at if we want to understand the logic of contemporary markets. It is, as we will discuss further in chapter 7, also a source for understanding the emergence of markets.

The bazaar is populated by traders, who are rivals and try to make money by trading with each other, and ultimately by selling to final consumers. It is fundamentally retail trading. The information advantage these professional traders have, as they know how much they paid for what they offer, will be used to increase their profit. It is the structural condition of their role as trader, and not as incumbents of the fixed-role of seller (or buyer), with the corresponding aim of "making money," which explains their unscrupulousness and lack of ethics (seen from the perspective of the buyer). The trader in the bazaar, according to Geertz, is not there primarily to build a brand, to establish long-term, trust-based relations, although this of course may be part of the game plan too. The aim is to make a "killing" instead of building up "a stable clientele or a steadily growing business," which means to "get as much as possible out of the deal immediately at hand" (Geertz 1963: 35).[2] The traders are tied to each other by credit relations, which cannot be separated from status relations.

Let us now turn to contemporary bazaars, which share many similarities, but in which the dealers are more fixed in the role of sellers. Bazaars, like those found in Istanbul, contain hundreds of stalls, which may continue also outside the formal, or physical, boundaries of the bazaar. A multitude of things are offered, and by walking through the alleys, the visitor is almost overwhelmed by the variety of scents and smells, everything from perfumes to spices, meat, and fish. Clothes, furniture, pots, shoes, tools, underwear, and much more are for sale. There is normally a spatial concentration, so that spices are sold in one area, and underwear in another. Products are on display, but not prices. Even though prices are provided on request, the process of arriving at a price that leads to a trade is like a ritual; this is one important cultural aspect of the bazaar, and how deals are closed may differ between different bazaars. There is, as it were, a price to be paid for concluding a transaction.

The culture of a bazaar includes how traders behave toward different types of buyer. One dividing line is between tourists/foreigners and locals. Foreigners are not likely to appear again and are also likely to possess less knowledge about prices, haggling, what to say or ask, whether one can enter a shop without buying, or whether one should accept an offer of tea, which is an important part of the culture of the market. Locals, in contrast, know how to do business in a bazaar economy and, although prices are lacking, they are at least partly known through gossip and experience. Nonetheless, what both foreigners and locals alike seem to share is the feeling that the lack of quoted prices means that they tend to pay more than they needed to.

The bazaar, with its concentration of trade, facilitates price comparisons, but the closeness of dealers also facilitates collaboration among them. The products that are for sale may appear similar. Product differentiation does occur, but the important thing is that it is not based on brand names. Some branded products are for sale, but the relevant shops are not marked and it may be difficult for an untrained eye to identify them.

Geertz (1992) has analyzed the role of the information and knowledge actors need when operating in the bazaar. To cope with uncertainty, which in this case is uncertainty concerning both what the market is all about – since "everything" is for sale – and the quality of what is offered, as well as the price, market actors build social bonds. Geertz calls this "clientelization" (1992: 228–9). The bazaar is a market place. But it is important to note that at least the modern bazaar is a market place which harbors several different "markets," such as markets for clothes, potatoes, knives, and many other things. It is a market place not least because there are other ways, such as the Internet and malls, of finding the same groceries and items for sale in the bazaar. To further clarify the distinction between a market and a market place, we will look at the stock exchange in the next chapter. There are, obviously, many other markets and market places that have been studied in detail by sociologists and other social scientists. But the bazaar is characterized by being both a final consumer market and a business-to-business market. In the bazaar we see traces of the old fair, and it is indeed an important case for anyone who wants to understand markets, whether historical or contemporary.

Summary

In this chapter, we have seen that a market can be rooted in the standards of its tacitly assumed goods. These goods may be co-determined by a technology (cf. Callon, Millo, and Muniesa 2007) for evaluating the offers, as is the case in the Brent crude oil market. The offers in a market can also be rooted in the status order of the market that "pumps out" the goods. This is the case in the consumer fashion market, with its rapidly changing products.

The analysis of social structure, culture, and value in this chapter are key to the analyses of the next two chapters. The distinctions between switch-role and fixed-role markets, as well as status and standard markets, are ideal-typical. Each form has a phenomenological and empirical counterpart. These distinctions are rooted in different forms of markets, and are not "perspectives" or "theories." There is, as we will see in the chapters to come, a correspondence between theories and markets, since some theories have been developed in relation to studies of certain kinds of markets. In chapter 5 we will look more closely at what we have called standard markets, followed by a discussion of status markets in chapter 6. This logic reflects the fact that it better accounts for the differences between markets than any other distinction.

5

Order out of Standard Offers

The distinction between standard and status markets was discussed in chapter 4. Standard markets are common, and this form can be observed in stock-exchange markets and markets for gold, crude oil, and in many other markets. In a standard market a scale of value serves as a valuation order regarding the product or service traded in the market. The corresponding everyday term is often quality. The main purpose of this chapter is to continue the discussion of standard markets, and to make it more concrete.

The rationale for the analysis in this and in the next chapter is to clarify how order is made, and specifically to clarify how the two important prerequisites are met and interrelated in standard markets. What is the offer (prerequisite 1)? And how does it get a price (prerequisite 3)? We will see that the relationship between the value of the offer, that is, what the offer "is," and the economic values, how much it is worth, differ between standard and status markets. This chapter discusses the neoclassical market model. The stock exchange is given special attention, as it is economically central, and because of its role for the development of the neoclassical market model. We will, in addition, discuss monopolistic competition and monopoly.

Order by Standard

Though order in any market is a combination of many factors, including the taken-for-granted background, we will zoom in on one principle of order in this chapter, namely, the offers and how they are standardized. We have defined standard negatively as being relatively more entrenched than the social structure (the status order), which means there are degrees to which standards are taken for granted, and thus degrees to which they order markets. Standard markets are defined positively as having a scale of value that serves as a valuation order regarding the offer of the market. Value is defined as the determination and rating of a "thing." The value, thus, does two different things: it establishes the offer, but it also makes it possible to "measure" offers according to the value. This means we can say that an offer is "more" or "less," or "better" or "worse," than another offer. A standard is simply a basis for evaluating things, and it does not imply that producers in a market offer identical products. Obviously, homogeneous products are one instance of standard markets. With the help of the standard, a vertical differentiation of offers can be created based on the standard (the value, or "quality scale," as some would say). The differentiation can be carried out with a continuous quality scale or one with discrete steps. A standard can be used for evaluation independently of the person's preferences, opinions, and judgments, though of course there may be opinions formed about the validity of standards.

How are standards generated? The standard, such as hardness of steel, or carats of diamonds (Bernstein 1992), may be generated within the market, or outside of it. The standard can be a decided principle of order, as when steel standards were internationally agreed upon, or they may evolve as an ordering principle due to mutual interaction, which most likely is the explanation of the standards traded in the global market of the "rights" to produce garments. Standard markets signal to sellers and buyers, to potential participants, as well as to those in other markets, what is valued, and the worth of the goods in the market. Hence, also, non-participants can judge the value of what they have, or what they want to trade, without taking part in the market, because it is possible to "measure" it against the standard.

Analytically, this valuation has nothing to do with price; it is merely a way of comparing what we have with the standard of the market, which is how prerequisite 1 is met. Below, we will study the relation between this standard and price-setting, which refers to how prerequisite 3 is met. However, the standard is a condition for transparent price-setting. Let us take an example: if it is unambiguous how to determine the "quality" of an offer, such as a 400 cubic meter of pine timber, this can be used to calculate prices. Quality may here refer to how old, dense, thick, and straight the stocks are, indicating their usefulness for different purposes. Prices are not consequences of quality, since quality as such says nothing about economic value, but there is a correlation between price and quality. Thus, as long as there is a market for pine timber, it is also possible to calculate the economic worth of timber that is standing in the forest (given that we know the quality of the trees).

If all input markets, and also the output markets, were standard markets, an economic actor may, at the least theoretically, calculate the profit rate for entering the market. This is how Hayek, Walras, and others, who think of the economy as one large market, envision the ideal situation: "the whole world may be looked upon as a vast general market made up of diverse special markets" (Walras 1954: 84). If knowledge of production is codified and prices are known, calculations would be enough to evaluate the situation. This, however, is rarely the case in the economy.

We have said that there is a correlation between the standard and price. If there is no correlation we do not have a standard, or we can say that we have a standard, but that it has nothing to do with what is valued in the market. The important point here, of course, is not whether there is a standard in an "objective," or in a hypothetical sense, but if there is an actual market standard in operation. To clarify this we can turn to George Akerlof (1970), who has identified the problem faced by buyers of used cars. It can be assumed that a seller of a used car knows its quality, but how can a potential buyer know this? This, Akerlof says, the buyer cannot know, since the asymmetric information relationship between buyers and sellers in the market is the problem. Buyers are not willing to pay the premium that, if they had as much knowledge as the seller, a good car is worth, since they do not know if they will get a good car or a lemon (a bad car). Price, as a consequence, tends to be close to what the average car is worth.

If we apply our concepts to the market for used cars, we see that there is no independent scale of value (in addition to year of production of the car and other obvious aspects) to separate cars of the same model. This means that buyers may either invest in huge search costs to find out the quality of the car, or of those cars that they see as the most attractive alternatives (and they would still not know how good these were compared to the other cars in the market). A consequence, according to Akerlof, is that sellers of good cars stay out of this market since they do not receive the payment they think they should for their cars.

But let us look at the alternatives for handling the problem of asymmetric market information, and here it is never a bad idea to keep one eye on reality. To overcome this problem, private sellers who, for example, put their cars for sale on the Internet, can do little to appear as a trustworthy car seller since selling a car is often a rare event, and a non-professional seller cannot build up a record of accomplishment. In other words, buyers cannot separate trustworthy identities from those who are not.

Firms offering used cars, however, can create identities in the market, since they repeatedly buy and sell cars. By gaining an identity in the market, as a dealer who is "fair" and who offers warranties that cover malfunctions of the car, it is possible to charge higher prices, and also to differentiate prices of the different cars the company has for sale. Akerlof points at "brand names" as a "counteracting institution" to overcome the uncertainty (Akerlof 1970: 499–500). The decision to buy a car can thus be guided by the status of the dealer, rather than the car as such. The dealer's identity is a signal (Spence 1979; White 1981, 2002b) of status in relation to other dealers and, of course, of the individuals trying to selling their cars. The cost of a search is higher if all individual cars have to be searched than if the sellers' status can be a proxy of the "quality" of the cars. If status becomes the dominating principle of order we have a status market.

To understand the difference between status and standard markets, we must include both cognition and temporality. As long as there is a standard, there is no limitation to the number of offers, as all can be judged easily. Status markets, in contrast, cannot exist if there are too many companies to keep track of: neither will it work when buyers of cars appear infrequently in the market, and thus "forget" how to grasp the status order. We have now discussed a non-homogeneous product, used cars. The situation would of course be different with new cars, in which all cars of the same brand and model are, at least arguably, of the same quality. In this case, the category would be homogeneous, but the problem here is to evaluate the differences between various brands and models in this market characterized by monopolistic competition.

Price, consequently, is not enough for evaluating if this is attractive for the sellers to put their assets on the market, and for the buyers to invest, as soon as we have goods that are not perfectly homogeneous. If a person owns a small one-bedroom property close to New York University, there will most likely be enough market transactions, and enough price information so that the person will know with some accuracy the value of her property. This is obviously on the basis of all this information being made available. The average price per square meter or square foot, when it goes up or down, is informative of the market trend, and this may be the best way of knowing the value of your home, or guessing what a home would cost to buy. Obviously, the style, the quality of the material, the exact location, the number of rooms, if it is on the ground floor, or has a balcony or an elevator, will matter, which is to say that properties are not homogeneous. Moreover, properties are different enough so that an auction, in one way or the other, is often the preferred method of transaction. Nevertheless, this is still a standard market, and not a status market.

In the property business, however, there is often a need for appraisals, that is, a detailed study of the object to find out its market value, but not as a technical investigation. The appraisal will shed light on the relationship between theoretical market value and actual market value of the property in question. The aim of the valuation is to estimate what a property would cost had it been sold in the open market, with competing buyers and sellers. It may come as a surprise that in some countries, like the US, banks decide if, and how much, to lend to customers on the basis of the appraisal reports. Moreover, if the actual market price is higher than the one stated by the appraisal, the bank may nonetheless base the credit to the customer on the appraisal and not on the actual market price because of a real deal involving a real buyer and a real seller. This suggests, in a slightly paradoxical way, that the bank uses the appraisal to judge the market value instead of the recorded market price of the transaction. This is because the value that is used in appraisals is assumed to be the average result if the valued object was sold repeatedly, though this is often based on a comparison with similar objects recently sold in the market. In other words, the market price the appraisal refers to is a theoretical market price. Theoretical ideas of markets have impact on real markets in this case. The real markets are, so to speak, based on the theory.

What, then, if the product offered in the market is perfectly homogeneous, such as shares of a company that are traded on the New York Stock Exchange? In such cases, an owner of shares has only to check the price that is presented on the Internet or in the daily newspaper to see the value of her portfolio. Alfred Marshall states this clearly: ""Any one share or bond of a public company, or any bond of a government is exactly the same value as any other of the same issue: it can make no difference to any purchaser which of the two he buys" (Marshall 1961: 326–7), because the goods are "absolutely standardized" (Marshall 1920: 319). In this case, the standard is the definition of the stock, a standardized contract, and there is no need to first judge the quality of the stock – since all are by definition identical – and then look for the price. The prices in the market contain all the information that is needed. In this market it does not matter with whom you trade, which is a condition for "anonymous" trading, and obviously for an automatic trading system.

Fixed- and Switch-role Markets

There are standard markets in which actors switch roles and those in which they enact only one of the two market roles. Let us begin by elaborating on a very common form of fixed-role market, namely, the labor market. Later in this chapter, we will analyze the stock exchange as an example of the switch-role market.

Labor markets

Labor markets are instances of fixed-role markets, in which the large majority of people appear as sellers in a labor market, and some of these are standard markets. The field called sociology of the labor market is large. However, given the relatively large importance of the field, and also some path-breaking studies, such as White's (1970) study on vacancy chains, and Granovetter's (1974) study on how to get a job, relatively little progress regarding labor markets has been made. This is not to deny other findings and discussion of the labor union (Streeck 2005), and the negotiation power of the two sides, employers and employees, of the market, the power of which has been crucial for shaping many societies in the West (Korpi 1983). The reason for the relatively weak situation theoretically, we claim, is that sociologists in this field, by and large, have taken over economic ideas and not developed sociological alternatives.

If one reviews the literature on markets, labor markets stand out as being "peculiar" or "special" (Swedberg 2003: 155). Though it may be existentially stressful to sell oneself as labor, since it is both emotionally, personally, socially, and economically central to most people, this is not to say that we need a separate market theory.

We propose that labor is an offer that can and should be understood with the tools developed in this book, and thus should account for much of the variation that we find when observing existing labor markets. This means that labor must be legitimate to trade, and today child labor is banned in many countries. Some labor markets, as we have made clear, are internal. We must, however, acknowledge the fact that labor as an "offer" has the capacity to change, disguise, resist, or innovate, aspects that are prominent, unlike the offers traded in markets for cows or cars.

Labor in some markets can, thus, be seen as standard offers. The condition for this requires there to be a standard according to which both sellers and buyers can evaluate the offers: how much am I worth in the market, or how much shall we pay for this person? We will see that in other labor markets, the ordering principle of status is more apt to account for what we observe.

The correlation between switch-role and standard markets

Switch-role markets are, empirically speaking, strongly correlated with standard products; or, put differently: there are few switch-role markets ordered by the principle of status. The reason, we propose, is that switch-role markets can only deal with already existing goods. The sociological account we have developed, however, does not start with such an assumption; what we call "offers" have to be studied and, as we will see, the large majority of markets are fixed-role markets. If the offer is taken for granted, in the sense that it exists prior to its introduction to the market, there is no need for the seller or buyer to change it or revise the object. The object is essentially kept as it is; it is only "exchanged" in the market. Hence, there is no constitutive relation between the seller or the buyer and the offer.

If you, in contrast, go to a concert to listen to Madonna, this offer cannot be separated from Madonna; it is not the same thing if you get to listen to Pink or to a recording by Madonna. The ticket for the concert, in contrast, can be bought from any source as long as the ticket is valid. Moreover, the house sold by a certain broker is not fundamentally altered by who is the selling broker. A property in a dodgy area is still dodgy regardless of whether the broker is a high-status broker or not. The reason for this "tipping point" between the centrality of the offer and the centrality of the actors is simply the question of which meaning is the most entrenched: the meaning of the actors' identities and their roles (the social status) or the objects (the standards).[1]

This tipping point is related to the constitution of objects traded in markets. We are dealing with two different value problems that are often mixed up in empirical research. One is the question of what is traded (prerequisite 1), and the other is the economic value of the object (prerequisite 2). The second problem of economic value is thus contingent on already "existing" and "defined" objects.

How can different markets solve these problems? A switch-role market can generate economic values but not constitute the objects. How are objects constituted? The offers, be it material or immaterial rights, are made and sanctioned by an authority, or they are taken for granted (constituted outside of the market). The constitution of objects must be understood in relation to their positioning in the web of meaning. The constitution of an object can thus be understood only in relation to other objects. A central aspect of the switch-role markets is this disconnection between the offers and those who trade in the market. A standard market with switch-roles detaches the identity of the market actors from the offer. Consequently, the fundamental constitution of the object in a switch-role market can only be made by organization (decided order), since this form of market implies no ties between offers, or between other offers and traders or between traders. This idea is implicit in the neoclassical model, but the model cannot account for the large number of markets in which what is offered is constituted by their relation to the producer, and often also to the consumers.

Neoclassical Market Theories

The neoclassical market theory is an instance of switch-role markets. The theory takes off from a positivistic standpoint rooted in ontological realism (Blaug 1992; Hausman 1992; Rosenberg 1992). This also explains why this theory takes the world, including the objects of trade in markets, for granted. The approach is deductive, and lack of data is seen as one reason to draw conclusions about reality based on theoretical assumptions of man and reality (Varian 1996: 240).

This market theory has its origin in the theories developed by classical economists, above all Leon Walras (1834–1910), and later codified in the works of Knight and Samuelson. Though it is often said that Walras developed one auction theory, he has, in fact, described five types of markets (Walker 1996). Furthermore, though sociologists and others sometimes behave as if there is one economic market theory, called the neoclassical market theory, it is clear that this is not correct, not the least since there are different cultures of economic reasoning in different countries (Fourcade 2009).

Today, economics students are by and large not exposed to the classical economic ideas, and few read Marshall and Walras. Backhouse observes that "Economists, by and large, do not take a serious interest in the history of their discipline" (1996: 7). Thus, the closer we get to the students of today, the more similar are the textbooks, and it is therefore not wrong to look at these books to find the "standard" theoretical model; a model that most economists have internalized in the socialization process of becoming economists. It is, in Thomas Kuhn's terms (1962), a paradigmatic science with a set of core concepts that are more or less taken for granted – among them, the idea of the market.

Though the focus here is not to analyze this theory in detail, it is useful to clarify some of the common assumptions of the theory. In most economics textbooks (e.g., Lipsey 1990), it is easy to find the core assumptions of the market theory. A similar list is found, for example, in the important book by Frank Knight (1921: 76–81). The list below comes from different sources, though it is possible to discuss each assumption in more detail:

- Actors are assumed to behave rationally and thereby know the consequences of their actions.
- Each actor is an atom who acts independently of others and is indifferent about with whom she interacts.
- Each actor's influence is limited, and is thereby without power to influence the market.
- Transaction costs are zero, and there is free entry and exit in the market. This also includes the fact there are no patents.
- Products in markets are homogeneous.

- The market is the only way of acquiring goods.
- The system is stable in relation to external shocks.

To make this more concrete, we look closer at the stock exchange, which was the source of inspiration and reference for the theories developed by Walras and Marshall.

The Stock Exchange

Even if some market theorists assume that the market emerged naturally, the theory of the market is not the result of a natural process. The market theory is not a mysterious and theoretical construction that we are dealing with, but an abstraction based on observation of real markets.

Walras developed his market theory in relation to actually existing markets (Kregel 1998). Though Walras's theoretical and abstract model may seem unrealistic, one may, in the words of Schumpeter, "learn from Marshall how to put flesh and skin on Walras's skeleton" (Schumpeter 1981: 1015). One reason for this need is that Walras's market model, or at least one of his theories, presumes an imaginary auctioneer (cf. Schumpeter 1981: 1002). However, Walras had analyzed, and above all experienced, the real economy long before he turned to economics. This experience, according to Jaffé's foreword to Walras's "Elements", comes from his many works as "a journalist, a clerk in a railway office, a managing director of a Bank for co-operatives, a newspaper editor, a public lecturer, and a bank employee" (Jaffe, in Walras 1954: 6).

How did Walras proceed when he developed his market theory? Walras is clear about where we shall find evidence of how market works: "Let us go into the stock exchange of a large investment centre like Paris or London" (Walras [1926] 1954: 84). We have previously shown that the early stock exchanges were houses for regulated trading of shares in different companies. At the stock exchange we find a fairly similar story (Weber 2000): market actors are price-oriented. We shall not repeat here what Weber and others have done, namely, to describe the stock exchange and how it works.

Also contemporary sociologists have studied stock exchanges, and this is often ethnographic work. Charles Smith (1981) shows, following a thread that goes back to Pareto, how market actors are categorized into different types. Among these types, some are more skilled than others, and some even possess information. Thus, traders have "customers," that is, investors, who provide the stock broker "with his living," but they are also – especially if they are well connected – a source of information to the broker (C. Smith 1981: 36). Mitchel Abolafia has studied traders in three financial markets, of which one is the stock market. Abolafia (1996) focuses on "market makers," that is, those in financial markets who trade to make money, and who make sure there are selling and buying prices for assets. Daniel Beunza and David Stark (2003) have studied the role of organization of the trading room for decision-making and collective response to external shocks. Brooke Harrington (2008) analyzed how small investors jointly, in so-called investment clubs, make decisions and interpret the stock exchange. Alex Preda has investigated the history of investors (Preda 2005), and also the role of financial markets, more broadly (Preda 2009). Wayne Baker (1984) has shown that network patterns emerge also in these "rational markets." Donald MacKenzie has in numerous publications analyzed stock exchanges and how they were made (e.g., MacKenzie 2006, 2009; MacKenzie and Millo 2003; MacKenzie, Muniesa, and Siu 2007a, 2007b). There are, of course, yet others who have written on aspects of the stock exchange, but many sociologists have, like the economists, taken the market for granted, and though it may appear important to show that the economy is also social – but what else could it be? – the social "add on" to what economists have made cannot represent a sociological foundation of a market theory.

Markets in Markets

The stock market is probably as close as a real market gets to the neoclassical competitive market. It is, for example, extremely fast; in the automatic trading system a deal can be executed within

250 microseconds. This section uses the theoretical tools we have developed to ask a simple question: is the stock exchange one market or does each individual stock represent an own market? Are the different stock exchanges that list the firms' shares best seen as one market or several different markets?

Let us begin with an observation. The stock exchange in Frankfurt, Börse Frankfurt, is different from the New York Stock Exchange, which is different from NASDAQ. In fact, these different stock exchanges compete with one another, all of them wanting to attract companies to be listed (traded) on their exchange. Thus, the stock exchanges operate on one market, the market for stock exchanges, or the market for stock market companies. These companies offer a market place and organize the trade (as sellers), and the individual firms are customers (buyers) that are listed to enable trade of their shares and to have access to capital for further investments. A company may be listed on several stock exchanges. The listed firms compete for capital with other companies on the market for investors. On this market, which is still often called a market place, the companies that run the stock exchanges also compete for capital with one another, and hence they may be listed on their own exchange. The only market prices we can observe on the stock exchange are those of shares of the different companies. Each day, or each second, when the stock exchange is open, the economic value of the different companies are set, since their shares are given prices in the double auctions in which investors enact, but frequently switch, the roles as buyer and seller. How are these different markets related?

Let us briefly look at these markets, and their interrelations. Though we say that the market is doing well when the Dow Jones Industrial Average is going up, this may say little about an individual stock, such as DuPont or any other of the 30 large companies of which the index of shares is composed. To say the market is "positive," or it is difficult to predict how it will behave in the next month or two, is common, but it is still the market trend, considered as an average of the listed companies to which we then refer. It is more correct to say that each individual stock company, such as IBM, DuPont, and Bank of America, is a market in its own right, since a company's shares, as Marshall stated, are a perfectly homogeneous product. In these different markets of individual stocks, the culture is identical, and the procedure is set in exactly the same way. How they differ is in the fact that they are about different things, since each company's stock is different from any other company's stock. The perception that there are different markets is strengthened by the observation that traders, investors, and analysts tend to focus on a few stocks, or a narrowly defined industry, or branch thereof. In this way, the difference between the different market places is reduced, in the eyes of investors, to a question of efficiency of executing orders and the correlated question of order volume (liquidity of stocks).

The stocks are traded by brokers who have the right to trade on a stock exchange. Only those being "members," defined as those having the proper license given by the stock exchange, are allowed to operate in the market as brokers. A transaction typically involves one investor selling and one buying, each of whom is represented by a broker who is trading. Hence, brokers face their customers as sellers of services in a fixed-role market for trading services. Brokers may, however, offer their customers online services, on which stock exchange a customer's order will be traded. A broker, to continue, switches role, between acting as "buyer" and "seller" on behalf of their customers in the stock exchange, and profits from the volume of the trade regardless of whether the stocks are going up or down.

Not only stocks, but also antiquities, can best be understood when we think of them as many different markets, though traded in one place (or one site on the Internet). Different auction houses compete with each other to sell essentially the same objects. Market categories on eBay, or any other electronic market place, indicate that we are talking here about different markets – all located in one market place. We should note a difference, however, between stocks traded every second on the stock exchange and antiques, which may, especially in the case of unique objects, reappear – if at all – extremely infrequently. This absence of continuous trading and the fact the objects are more or less unique, among other things, means there are few prices quoted that can be used for comparison and makes it much harder to know the values of the items prior to the auction. There is thus a distinction to be made between one-shot auctions and repeated auctions (Krishna 2009). This affects the predictability of the markets.

We can observe here what has already been argued in chapter 2: markets are embedded in each other. Though each financial market is embedded in a larger context of institutions and life-world, it may be more important for our understanding to know how they are embedded in each other (White 2002b). We have now studied the most well-known form of market, the auctions that take place in the stock exchange. Next, we turn to markets in which competition is not "perfect" as it is represented in the neoclassical market model.

Differentiation and Fixed Roles – Monopolistic Competition

The roots of what is called monopolistic competition are Marshall's discussion of imperfect competition and Chamberlin's discussion of monopolistic competition, both of whom are refer-ring to markets in which producers differentiate their offers. To this, we may add the discussion of oligopolistic competition, which refers to markets with a small number of sellers holding a fixed role, but with identical or almost identical products. Economists are aware of the fact that the neoclassical model is limited to a small number of markets. Paul Samuelson is clear about this: "our curves of supply and demand [i.e., the core of the perfect market model] strictly apply only to a perfectly competitive market where some kind of standardized commodity such as wheat is being auctioned by an organized exchange" (Samuelson 1969: 69). He sees the Chicago exchange as one such example. Others have been more explicit about the rare cases of "pure" or "perfect" competi-tion. Frank Knight says: "in view of the fact that practically every business is a partial monopoly, it is remarkable that the theoreti-cal treatment of economics has related so exclusively to complete monopoly and perfect competition" (Knight 1921: 193). In reality, we seldom observe indifferent economic actors and homogeneous products. Differences between offers and tradesmen are almost always present: "be it personally, reputation, convenient location, or the tone of his shop, differentiates the thing purchased to that degree, for what is bought is really a bundle of utilities, of which these things are a part" (Chamberlin 1948: 8). Chamberlin argues that there are degrees of competition; between "sport roadsters and ten-ton trucks" (Chamberlin 1948: 9) it is virtually zero, but we can easily see that there is competition between different sports cars, such as Lamborghini and Ferrari.

Product differentiation and branding result in differences in the eyes of consumers. Though the products are similar enough for consumers to see them as alternatives, and for producers to see other producers as competitors, they are different enough to avoid an economic "war" in which all producers compete with one another. Competition is limited to producers that are offering relatively similar products or services.

With the introduction of monopolistic competition, several central assumptions of the neoclassical model are revised. Economic actors are not treated as atoms since producers orient to one another (Chamberlin 1948: 51–3). The second major change is that products are no longer homogeneous. There are different ways to create a market niche for a producer, such as patent, differentiating the product, and differentiating the context and conditions of sale. Differentiating is based on the "characteristics of the product itself, such as exclusive patented features; trade market; trade names; peculiarities of the package or container, if any; or singularity in quality, design quality or style. It may also exist with respect to the conditions of sale" (Chamberlin 1948: 56). In consumer markets, it is easy to identify markets in which firms differentiate their products by "branding" (Lury 2004) which has already been observed by Marshall (1920: 300–2). Market niches are created (cf. Coase 1988: 37; Kirzner 1973: 137–8) by rivaling firms that are related via competitive relations in the market (Burt 1992).

These firms do not thereby create absolute monopolies, even if a firm has a patent; they are viewing each other as competitors and are seen as competitors by the consumers. It is nonetheless clear that product differentiation in one way diminishes the competitive pressure, and by creating brands firms protects themselves since the uncertainty is decreased, both for firms and their customers. It is an efficient way for producers compared with price competition: "as a bombardment is in comparison with forcing a door" (Schumpeter 1975: 84). Producers not only have to cut prices to compete; they may in fact raise prices if customers are willing to pay for premium goods (cf. Veblen 1953). Many of the commodities that used to be "homogeneous," or at least not branded, such as butter, milk, bread, and much more have over time become branded. Hence, for consumers, monopolistic competition offers a way of creating distinctions, and for producers less risk and more predictability since they at least can protect a brand or, as we will say, control their identity. With this insight, we may ask if the aim of a firm might be to have a full monopoly?

Out of the Market – Monopoly – Back into the Market

Monopoly, oligopolistic competition, and monopsony are deviant cases of the perfect model.[2] Economists tend to speak of monopoly markets (e.g., Stigler and Sherwin 1985: 557), but anyone who has ever played the game Monopoly knows when there is one winner: one person controls the city and has eliminated all other competitors for the ownership of property. The winner is then in the position to maximize his income from those who want to use these properties because of his position. In fact, it may appear that even the smallest child who masters the game knows more than the professional economists, as the latter keeps talking of a market even after the essential elements of competition are eliminated. Furthermore, the interest of any economic actor in a producer market is not to cultivate markets, but to eliminate competition. Though the ideology of the market calls for "rhetorical" statements by participants in markets, such as "it is good for us with competition," life would be easier and the profit higher if the company was in a monopoly situation. In reality, few cry if their competitors have to exit the market, due to political regulation or to competitive pressure. Furthermore, espionage and other means of non-market competition exist in markets to outperform rivals, in addition to pure market competition.

Collaboration is another way for economic actors to overcome the competitive pressure and survive in the economy (Fligstein 2001: 71). Collaboration in the form of networking, such as networks of information sharing among owners of hotels (Ingram and Roberts 2000), or even as formal organizations in a market, is of course easier when few actors are involved. Corruption (Granovetter 2007) is another possible outcome when actors try to create and maintain monopolies.

If there is only one seller and no competition, we have a monopoly. We have also stated that a market must be about one thing (and not everything). In this sense, a monopoly means there is only one seller of the goods in question. If the seller is not raising the price, and there is no shortage of what is being offered, we have exchange with multiple buyers – all consumers can purchase as much as they want at the given price. In this case, there is a monopoly but no market, since there is no competition.

But if we return to our market definition and what we said above, there can also be competition when there is only one seller, as long as the buyers compete *on the market* for the offers. If bread is for sale at a fixed price, but the number of loaves is limited, a situation that was not uncommon in former Eastern communist countries with commando economy, buyers may compete for a position in the line at the bakery. This is clearly a situation where there is competition for bread, but it is, as it were, a struggle that is solved among the buyers, and not across the market. The buyers can do nothing, if the bakery operates as a bureaucracy, to persuade the bakery to sell them more, or before other customers are allowed to purchase. Hence it is not market competition.

Market competition, to recall, exists if the bakery instead sells their limited supply of loaves through an organized auction. In this way, they make use of their market power to increase their revenue. Buyers enter into a struggle with each other, but not with fists to get a good position in the queue (as this would violate the condition that market interaction is peaceful), but with their money (or other equivalent economic resources) to close deals. In this way, the monopoly power of the seller is used to create competition among the consumers. When this is the situation, we can talk of a monopoly market. This is the case since we meet the minimal condition of the market, that there is competition on one of the two sides.

Summary

In this chapter, we have discussed and studied standard markets. Because of the frequency with which the neoclassical economic market model exists, we have spent some time presenting and analyzing this model. This is not only an instance of a standard market, but also of a switch-role market. Hence, the neoclassical model does not account for the many markets in which actors are identified with one side of the market. We will therefore return to the discussion of consumers and producers in chapter 6.

The neoclassical theory is a useful tool for understanding some markets, but not others. It follows that those who propagate for this market model as a universal solution of all economic coordination problems may do so for ideological or paradigmatic-scientific reasons (Kuhn 1962), rather than with the ambition to rethink what we "know." The sociology of science perspective that has been used to understand not only the economy, but the way knowledge is produced, sedimented, and applied, is of large importance (e.g., Callon 1998b; Callon, Millo, and Muniesa 2007; MacKenzie 2006, 2009; MacKenzie and Millo 2003). This form of analytical reflection, which includes taking the theory apart, but which also includes the reflection on the consequences of scientific knowledge production, is of crucial importance for highlighting the role and impact that economic reasoning has had on social life.

It is clear that the theory of monopolistic competition is a major step forward to obtain a better understanding of the real economy and its markets. These ideas were central to White, as we will see in the next chapter, and in all these models we find that market actors are powerful and that each may affect the market. This is obviously the case in monopoly markets. Power is thus an essential component in most real markets. There are, moreover, two things that we have to return to in chapter 6. The first is the underlying idea of quality as part of the differentiation between producers. How shall we account for differentiation when there is no way to adjudicate quality differences?

6

Order out of Status

In the previous chapter, we studied markets ordered through the principle of standard. We also saw how the assumption of a homogeneous product, as used in the neoclassical economic market model, is covered by the notion of standard market. This means that actors can calculate and predict their actions without having to focus on the offers as such, since they are given, and it is a precondition for the pure theory of competition that enables actors to focus on price. The purpose of this chapter is to relate standard and status markets, with a focus on the latter.

Those operating in real markets know that economic actors, firms and humans, rarely compete with identical products by using only price as a means. Investment banks, carpenters, sociologists, and fashion brands offer differentiated offers in their respective markets. But, as was shown, product differentiation would also be covered by the notion of the standard market if the different offers could be evaluated against a market standard. As long as this is possible they compete along several dimensions, of which price is only one.

In this chapter, we shall look at markets in which there is no standard against which market actors can evaluate the offers. How is order maintained in such cases? This chapter studies markets in which the social status order is the most entrenched social construction. This means that order in this market is not derived from the offers but from those who act in the market. We will also discuss borderline cases. We have deliberately decided to present White's theory of producer market here, to make it easier to identify his contribution. It is, moreover, against the background of White's theory that we will look more closely at status markets.

Differentiation of Goods and Identities

If economists have focused on markets with homogeneous products and in which actors switch roles, sociologists have formed their market view based on the works of Harrison White. His model should be seen as sociological manifestation of ideas of product differentiation that we have identified in the works of Marshall and Chamberlin. White shifts, one may say, the focus from the products to the producers. His theory, interpreted with the concepts of this book, is a standard market in which actors holds fixed roles. White's theory of markets is an instance of his general theory, which, in brief, states identities try to control their environment. The environment is largely made up of other identities (cf. Azarian 2003; White 1992, 2008). The producer market is a special case of the social formation that White calls interface (White 1993). This is characterized by matching between producers and customers across the interface (market), and is disciplined by quality.

Harrison White's market theory aims at explaining the markets that are in the majority; markets he calls production markets (White 2002b). The neoclassical market theory, White says, fails to account for two key aspects of production markets: the way that firms move to conquer and maintain market shares in a specific market (White 1981: 517–18, cf. 541), and the fact that the number of firms in a market rarely exceeds a "dozen or so." White defines markets as "self reproducing social structures among specific cliques of firms and other actors who evolve roles from observing each other's behavior" (White 1981: 518). His theory focuses on the production flow in which chains of the market pump products downstream, until the transformed products reach the final consumers. An important aspect of this is that each

producer market is a tripartite distinction of suppliers (sale), producers (transformation), and buyers (procurement), and therefore
it has "two distinct possibilities for a market interface. These are
upstream orientation toward suppliers and downstream orientation toward consumers" (White 2002b: 11, cf. 213). White sees
the market as an interface in which producers are "jockeying for
positions," meaning that the market is made up of producers who
hold positions that are relative to each other (White 1993: 166). In
White's theory, producers, essentially seen as rational actors, are
oriented to each other, and this is the key point for understanding competition, market boundaries, and the role of consumers.
He has developed a mathematical model, but this is rooted in the
phenomenology of market actors' everyday experience.

White identifies the two sides, or two roles, we observe in any
market: producers and consumers. Producers permanently enact
the role as sellers in this market, and they thereby gain their identities. A central feature is that the producers differentiate among
themselves and, according to White, this is the drive for market
emergence. Thus, product differentiation, and therefore identity
differentiation of the producers, are mutually constituting (White
and Eccles 1987: 985). White says: "in a given market, each
producer firm will have a position that is entirely relative to the
position of other producers in that market, as perceived by and
across all of those whom they jointly supply" (White 1993: 164).
Producers relate themselves to each other; or, as White and Eccles
express it, producers' "primary focus is each other" (White and
Eccles 1987: 984).

Firms positions themselves in niches, and by entrenching themselves they acquire identities (White 2002a). Firms try to control
their identities, but this can only be done in relation to their environment, most notably other producers, who also try to control
their niches and identities. It is through this process, according to
White, that the social role structure of the producers is constructed.
The collective identities of producer markets, to be seen as mol-
ecules made of up of atoms (firms), means that they are embedded
in an environment of other markets. Within the market, "Firms
shelter themselves within the rivalry of a production market"

(White 2002b: 13), essentially by carving out niches through the means of branding. The production of a market, White notes, is an unintended consequence of this "internal" orientation among the producers (White 1993: 168). We may, so far, draw the conclusion that producers are obsessed with each other – do consumers not play a role?

It is correct to say that White's theory is primarily occupied with the producers' side, but it should be underlined that the consumers' side intimately affects what producers do; and in this sense the consumers play a central role in his theory (e.g., White 1988). Consumers, according to White, do not know each other; nor do the producers know them. Consumers discriminate between the different producers in the market "in ways summed up as quality, but no one can quantify this in advance or independent of volumes shipped" (White and Eccles 1987: 984). The consumers can say "yes" or "no" to what the producers offer, that is, the terms of trade of the producers. White sees a trade-off within the market function, which is expressed in the following way: revenue (W) as a function of the shipped volume (y). The terms of trade, seen from the perspective of the producers, are the revenues received for the various volumes shipped by the different firms operating in this particular market (White and Eccles 1987: 984). It is this quality discrimination that produces the curve of the producers' pecking order.

Some producers offer high-quality items and sell them for more money, and usually fewer items than those of lower quality that ship larger volumes. Firms may also differ on the input side, due to abilities, being affected, for example, by the costs of production (White 1992: 43). Furthermore, the cost structure of firms may differ, for example, due to the quality and character and the location of their plants. Consumers react passively to the acts of the producers. They react to what White calls the quality of the products, since the consumers can compare the commodities with the commodities of other producers. It is through this process, according to White, that the social structure of the market is constructed.

Quality is related to what is in "the eye of the beholder" (White 1981: 522). The notion of quality in White's model "relies on standings that ... emerge from interactions among judgments by both producers and consumers," which reflects the situation "[i]n actual business life" where, White continues, "quality meanings become jointly imputed to properties that have gotten bundled together as a 'product,' even though these properties may seem to have an observer various and somewhat arbitrary" (White 2002b: 10). It must be stressed that White is talking about a dual differentiation of quality, which refers both to product and producer, but this nonetheless boils down to a "quality index" (White 2002b: 10). This may become "reified during the evolution of an industry." It may also be organized "by a trade association," and such "index can become taken for granted so that it functions, like the IQ index, as a particular numerical scale that is widely accepted, by participants and observers alike" (White 2002b: 78). We should, consequently, not think of quality as intrinsic to the products. Nonetheless, quality, or as we would say, standard, is White's way of meeting the first prerequisite, what the market is all about.

How do producers gain knowledge? One reason for the preoccupation of the firm with its "competing" firms is that their behavior and what can be learned from this is an important source of knowledge. The producers see themselves and their competitors in the "mirror" of the market, which reflects producers' decisions and their outcomes, but the producers cannot see through the mirror to the customers (White 1981: 543–4). It is "a mirror," as White says, since the result of the interaction with the customers is only seen after the firm has presented its own terms of trade to the customers. From this perspective, supply and demand are simply by-products of the process of finding and reproducing identities in the market.

The information necessary for the decisions of a firm, for example, the situation of the market, the positions of the other firms in the market, and so on, comes not only from observations within the market itself, but is also obtained "over luncheons with others in the trade, from trade associations, from one's own customers, and so on" (White 1981: 519). White has later called this "gossip" (White 1993: 167). He consequently assumes that the producers are well informed and know of their competitors. Knowledge is key for defining market boundaries: the producers, by knowing the market, can tell who is in the market and who is not (White and Eccles 1987: 985). Gossip, as well as the established "rules of the game" (White and Eccles 1987: 984), suggest that White's approach accounts for the second market prerequisite, namely, the culture of the market.

Price-setting is a central activity in markets, and the third prerequisite that must be met in order to have an ordered market. Prices are set in relation to the relative competition of the producers within a market, according to White. The profit may be higher in some markets than in others, that is, the absolute level of price cannot be affected by the actors themselves within the market; only the relative prices are part of what can be negotiated. Service and transaction costs may also be the result of historical traditions. As White and Eccles phrase it: "prices are not something that mysteriously emerge from 'the market'. They are part of the terms-of-trade and are socially constructed by the actors involved in the exchange" (White and Eccles 1987: 985).

The market, according to White, is a social construction which is unintended and self-reproducing; producers reproduce the niches they have created. All market actors share the same perception of the market in which they are active. When the actors orient themselves in this way, they also reproduce the "social fact" of the market (White 1988: 227–9). Given what actors know, they tend to make use of the knowledge of the last period, and essentially repeat their actions, which of course reaffirm the present order. Hence, White stresses the order of the market and the reproduction of such actions, rather than dynamics, innovation, and radical change, and argues that "Market transactions deal with repetitive rather than one-shot production" (White 2002b: 9–10). But not only is the market reproducing itself; also the actors reproduce themselves in the network of interaction that makes up the market (White 1995: 67–71). On a more general level, White is talking about a social order driven by a wish for control of identities, and this produces a pecking order (White 1992). The market phenomenology, in which firms signal differences that can be discerned by consumers with limited cognitive capacity, and the idea that the market is a pecking order are the reasons why the number of actors in producer markets is limited to "a handful or a dozen participants" (White 2002b: 10). White stresses that markets are embedded in each other (White 2002a), and it is clear his theory of production markets has been a starting point for sociologists who study markets, and we now turn to some of these.

Sociological production market studies

The importance of White for other sociologists studying the market is easy to realize when surveying the literature. This is particularly the case in the US. White has had an impact in two ways, as the modern father of network theory, and through his market theory which, of course, is underpinned by the idea of networks. Below, we give some examples of studies, in addition to those already mentioned throughout this book, which have made use of White's ideas of production markets.

Neil Fligstein draws on White's theory for his work on market making, but blends it with Bourdieu and his own work on organization to generate his own approach, called "market as politics." This idea has had a large impact in the field of economic sociology. To Fligstein the question of the institutional and cultural requirements of markets is central. To explain these, Fligstein argues, we must understand the connection between the state and market building. Fligstein, however, acknowledges that markets can be studied without reference to governments (Fligstein 2001: 12), but his major theoretical contribution is on the making of markets. Fligstein stresses the interplay in market construction between the state and, predominantly, organizations in what he calls "fields" (Fligstein 2001, 2008; Fligstein and Mara-Drita 1996; Hellman 2007). According to Fligstein, new markets are characterized by a form of politics that resembles "social movements"; each firm that takes part is trying to impose its "conception of control," but they may also form coalitions (Fligstein 2001: 76). Eventually, a market comes to be ordered (or stable, which is Fligstein's term). Fligstein's approach has been used to analyze European markets

(Fligstein 2008), but also, for example, employment systems and shareholder value (Fligstein 2001). Of course, there are other studies that are informed by White's approach, on minivans (Rosa, Porac, Runser-Spanjol, and Saxon 1999), or frozen pizzas, which is White's (1993) own example.

Economic Thinking

We have seen that early economic thinking focused on the product. The stock exchange was the empirical material for developing an economic market theory, which has a well-protected core (Lakatos 1970) which has remained basically unchanged since it was developed by Walras.

However, compared to neoclassical market theory, Marshall and Chamberlin made enormous progress by introducing the idea of product differentiation, and the idea of game theory represents an advancement since the phenomenology of most real producer markets has a limited number of actors who indeed orient to each other (Aspers, Kohl, Roine, and Wichard 2008). White's account of markets refers to a signaling-interpretation argument: neither producers nor consumers can keep track of too many actors, since the differences are no longer discernible. The orientation among producers is normally not included in economic models, since economists still treat each of these "monopolists" as small in relation to the market, and market is here "the economy." The introduction of the producer moves the focus from an abstract notion of competition, to a focus on the ways in which competitors are defined (Porac and Thomas 1990).

The literature we have discussed so far can be covered using the notion of standard markets. But what if there is no "quality" scale? That is, how do we manage when there is no way we can talk of products before we take them to the market? Furthermore, how can we conceptualize markets in which what is valued depends on the interaction of both types of market actors, that is, producers and consumers? We will see that we move from Knightian uncertainty, concerned with problems of economic value (prerequisite

3), to the more fundamental problem of ambiguity, meaning that what is traded is questioned (prerequisite 1).

Consumers, so far, have played a less prominent role, if considered at all. In what follows below, consumers will play a central role, and we will look at status markets, which represent another form of market. It should, however, be emphasized that status markets do not replace all other markets. The neoclassical model, for example, is the most accurate theory for understanding exchanges, but not other markets.

The role of status and identity in markets

We will now look at markets in which "status" is central. Many of the studies discussed in this section have used the Whitean framework. A large majority of them look at labor markets, and these studies frequently describe the intersection of identity, market, and evaluation. It is no surprise that many of these studies have zoomed in on aesthetic and creative activities, since this field makes clear what we can observe also in other parts of the economy: the focus is not on what is done, but on who is doing what. At the end of this chapter, we present the idea of status market.

Faulkner and Anderson (1987) have shown that market, mobility, and career are interconnected, in a study of the markets in the Hollywood film industry for projects (cf. Hirsch 1992). Careers involve a series of events that over time are tied to an identity. Identities gain, in this process, reputation in the market, which means we can talk of a "distinct industry identity" (Faulkner and Anderson 1987: 906). In this case, markets and careers intersect or, in other words, the market is the arena in which identities are made, evaluated, and thus make careers, and reputation is produced as people from both sides of the market interact. Faulkner and Anderson show that sellers with high credit seek buyers with good credit and that directors with good credit seek cinematographers with good credit (1987: 901). Ezra Zuckerman et al. (2003) have shown that workers in creative industries, such as movie actors, tend to become specialized because of how they are perceived by the other side of the market. This results in them doing similar things, which further reinforces their identities, supporting Faulkner's (1983) earlier work on film composers in markets.

Faulkner has, in a lesser-known study, shown the relation between producers and consumers of music, and what we should highlight is the consumers' role for the product's quality (Faulkner 1971: 108). Thus, Faulkner stresses the associative relation across the market, in which production includes both sellers and buyers (Aspers 2006: 12). The production in the "market," he says, is made collectively; a team joins up to perform music with a conductor. Faulkner has the following to say about the studio musician: "Like other free-lancers (writers, photographers, detectives), he competes for jobs in a market where his ability, reputation, tact and social contacts determine the nature and volume of his work. He is a musical entrepreneur – a musician for hire" (Faulkner 1971: 44). Faulkner, consequently, is studying a labor market, though composed of self-employed people.

Aspers (2006) has, in a study of fashion photographers, shown how their status is generated in the market for editorial fashion photography, and the status in this market positions them in a rank order that makes it clear who is "good" and who is less "good." The more status, the more money the photographer can make in the market for advertisement photographs. In this way, status in one market is translated into money in another. This is typical of many aesthetic markets (Aspers 2001: 1), reflecting their bipolar character between "art" and "economy" (Bourdieu 1996; Plattner 1996). Like Faulkner, Aspers studies self-employed people. Joanne Entwistle (2002) has studied fashion models, and in this labor market, too, there is an aesthetic evaluation of the models. Model agents evaluate the models, though the market always has the final say. The models, in one sense, have to be made, and thereby gain an identity and a position, which may later be turned into money in the markets where models are offered money. Olav Velthuis (2005) has studied pricing in the art market. This is a market in which there are no objective standards, and though Velthuis discusses cultural scripts of pricing, these scripts must be seen in the light of the positions actors hold in the social structure. In Velthuis's case, art objects are first made by their interaction with galleries and other institutions that bestow them with value, and only then can they be sold.

Joel Podolny's work is clearly influenced by White's market theory. The main difference is that he speaks of status as a proxy of quality, and says: "Like White, I conceptualize the market as a structure that is socially constructed and defined in terms of the perceptions of market participants, but my focus is not so much on roles as it is on status positions" (Podolny 1993: 830). Podolny argues that status generates a hierarchy among producers, and their positions affect their opportunities in the market. It is noteworthy that he follows White in focusing on the producers' side, and sees the differentiation of products as reflected in (status) positions. Status is defined as "the perceived quality of that producer's product in relation to the perceived quality of the producer's competitor's products" (Podolny 1993: 830). The main function of status is to signal the underlying quality of the products the firm produces (Podolny 2005). Status is affected by what the producers do, that is, the signaling effect is manipulated by the producer's way of producing and selling the product. Quality, he says, is unobservable "before the consummation of a transaction" (Podolny 1993: 830). Podolny does not entirely clarify the separation between actual and perceived quality, though he elaborates to some extent on the distinction. It is evident here, as in later texts by Podolny (Lynn, Podolny, and Tao 2009; Podolny and Hsu 2003), that he sees status as a proxy for objective quality.

Podolny (1994) indicates how quality may be related to status in markets. He argues that in markets where it is not easy to define the quality of products objectively, actors are faced with Knightian uncertainty (Podolny and Hsu 2003). To deal with uncertainty, actors seek those with whom they have interacted in the past, and they are also more likely to interact with firms of equal status to theirs (Podolny 1994: 459–61). Podolny connects status to what is produced by the producer and to the "exchange relations with consumers, ties to third parties associated with the market, and affiliations with other producers" (Podolny 1993: 833). This means that the social net of interactions with other producers and with consumers is important in determining how customers perceive the commodity or service in relation to those of other producers (Podolny 1994: 460).

Podolny argues that the producers form a status order, in which some producers have more status than others do. Prices follow from status: the more status, the higher the price. Status, Podolny (1993) says, can cut costs for producers in several ways. The producer is likely to receive more attention without having to pay for it, since people may talk and write about these products. High-status producers do not have to convince the consumers of their claims, which means they face lower transaction costs. High-status producers may also face lower costs when they obtain capital from banks. Finally, they may obtain a good working force for less money, as it is a popular work place, or seen as a place where people can learn things. Podony's model, moreover, is based on three assumptions: (1) that quality is unobservable; (2) that status is regarded as a signal of quality; and (3) that perceptions of a producer's status depend on the identity of those to whom the producer is tied.

Bourdieu informs us about an empirical case of how it matters who one is in the market, though he captures this in terms of symbolic capital. Bourdieu says: "Symbolic capital is valid even in the market. A man may enhance his prestige by making a purchase at an exorbitant price, for the sake of his point of honour, just to 'show he could do it'" (Bourdieu 1990: 119). It may, according to Bourdieu, be enough for a man with much social capital to show up with his face, in order to "come back with the whole market" (Bourdieu 1990: 119). Hence, symbolic capital can even be used as credit, which of course can only be granted to those who have the right credentials, or are known in the network or in the market, and only by those who recognize this type of social capital.

We have now, in several different markets, shown that quality and status appear to be interrelated. Art (cf. Beckert and Rössel 2004) and fashion markets are typical examples of markets in which status matters. Status matters in both producer markets and labor markets. Theoretically, we lack tools to account for this large set of studies. We will now turn to an attempt to address this issue, called status markets.

Status Markets

The model of status market aims to cover the above-discussed markets. Order in a status market is a result of the order of the social structure of the market, which is the structure of the identities of the two sides of the market: buyers and sellers. These two sets of identities are relatively stable social constructions. They are at least more stable than what is traded in the market, fashion garments. A status order lacks an independent principle of evaluation. This means that one cannot judge the value of a commodity outside the context of social interaction. Among status markets, as was done with standard markets, we can separate between fixed-role and switch-role markets. We begin by discussing fixed-role markets, in which producers gain identities as sellers and consumers as buyers.

Status markets partly constitute their objects of trade by gaining their meaning in the observable patterns of interaction between buyers and sellers. In status markets, buyers and sellers are known, at least as ideal-types. We saw that White's model assumes that the buyers are an anonymous mass, but in a status market it is necessary to separate the actors on each side from one another. This means that trading is largely public or, at the least, known to those in the market. What does "known" mean here? We are talking about identities, and, to recall, this is different from persons. We have seen that producers, as suggested by White, Podolny, and others, can create distinctions among themselves so that each gains a distinct market niche. The rank order of producers' status positions cannot include more identities (cf. brands) than consumers can distinguish between. This is the cognitive aspect of producer markets that we have mentioned previously.

Consumers must not appear as persons, but can be seen as ideal-typical. In the same sense that producers are different, ideal-typical consumers may be different. The sociological research on consumers in markets has not systemically been incorporated into market theories, though there is a large literature (e.g., Birtwistle and Shearer 2001; Fine and Leopold 1993; McCracken 1988; Miller 1987; Slater 1997; Southerton 2001; Zelizer 2005b). Pierre

Bourdieu (1984) has made a large study of consumers, showing that consumers are positioned in a relational space. Several activities, such as holiday, preferences for food, or knowledge of art, are tied together with positions so that the positions reflect different lifestyles. We should, in addition, mention Bourdieu's work on housing markets (Bourdieu 2005), which stresses the role of the state, and also how suppliers position themselves in relation to each other and the potential buyers. If we apply Bourdieu's approach to a single market, we can see that each ideal-typical identity, each consisting of a unique set of ties, tends to consume certain goods and reject others. Consumers are assumed to identify with, and to create themselves as a result of, what they do, including purchasing (Warde 1994).

Ranking of status orders

We have now, though briefly, discussed the two sides of fixed-role markets. How do these rank orders emerge? An important idea is that the status orders of one or both sides can be constructed in other markets or social formations. Order in different economic and non-economic evaluations may be interrelated. In this way, markets are not only embedded in other markets, but in non-economic valuation orders. Lucien Karpik (2010) has studied in detail the different judgment devices that help to bring order in status markets, such as branding, guides (like Lonely Planet), and the existence of established critics. In status markets, the role of critics may become central, since they provide "guides to current and future tastes" (Zuckerman 1999: 1406). These critics and others who fulfill the same task must not be part of the market.

Furthermore, a market may not mean as much to consumers, some of whom are infrequently taking part, as to the producers whose identities are essentially defined in "their" producer market, such as garment brands that gain their identities in the ready-to-wear segment. Consumers may be enthusiasts and truly commit themselves to certain lifestyles. But a lifestyle is often defined by the combination of things that are purchased in different markets.

Generally speaking, consumers as beings are not as tied to one specific market as are producers.

The status orders, that is, the rank order of the different identities that are part of the market, consisting of producers and consumers, may be the result of the interaction in one specific market. When high-status buyers and high-status sellers come together, high-status offers are made. Their interaction defines, as it were, the value of the offer in the market. When well-known actors wear designer garments on the red carpet at the Oscar awards, this reinforces the status of both the designers and the actors. Status, as Podolny (2005) says, leaks, so that a well-known star who wears a lesser-known designer's dress endows that designer with status, and vice versa.

In status markets, prices in terms of "money of accounts" do not reflect only the valuation of the items, since there is no independent scale of value. In this case, prices become epiphenomena of status. But the more uncertain the situation is, for example, if the status order is unclear, and if a new market emerges, the more likely it is that price, too, can become a signal of what is traded; price brings meaning to the product so that an expensive wine is "good" wine, to take one example. Our point is that prices in terms of money of accounts co-construct what is offered and the status of those who trade.

There are also status markets where actors switch roles, though they are probably less common. In such markets, actors with high status may consequently appear as either buyer or seller at a given moment in time. By appearing in the market they may affect the objects traded. In a certain way, the transaction in the Kula ring represents an example (though not of a market) of status exchange: necklaces once possessed by a king or any other high-status person have more value, and this has nothing to do with the "intrinsic" quality of the material objects.

The model of status market presented here (Aspers 2009b) suggests that both producers and consumers are important for constituting what is offered in the market or, better, it is in the act of transaction, and, later, when these goods or services are used so that the transaction is publicly known in the market, that the buyers endow the producers with status. In this case, both sides have to be "known," since status cannot be distributed anonymously. Evaluation is central, and the idea of how identities are generated in the market as a result of evaluation and transactions can be seen in other fields too, for example, in financial markets (Podolny 1993), markets for movie workers (Zuckerman, Kim, Ukanwa, and von Rittmann 2003), and in fashion (Aspers 2010).

Summary

With this chapter, we come to an end on our journey. We have developed tools for understanding markets. It is with the notions of order, either in the form of standard or of status, and the idea of identification and roles, and in the form of switch roles and fixed roles, that we have analyzed markets. The variations of everyday terms, such as product, consumer market, labor market, and monopoly markets – ways of making distinctions between markets – are descriptive, but not necessarily logical, and have been accommodated by a more abstract, but still more efficient, theoretical apparatus. A central idea is the difference between market forms.

To conclude, in this chapter we have taken the last step by introducing and presenting at length the idea of status markets. In chapter 3, the historical literature on markets was covered, but without really addressing the question of how market making can be theoretically accounted for. This question, from a logical point of view, can only be addressed once we know what a market is, and of which form of market we are talking. It is to this central question of market making we now turn.

7

Making and Controlling Markets

It is only after we have clarified what is a market, and how markets have developed historically, that we can explain the principles for market making. Markets are made, though this is not to say that they are always made by design. In reality, markets are made in social processes by combining and creating elements and by meeting the prerequisites we have discussed, what the market is about, how to act in markets, and how prices are set. The task of the social science is primarily to provide ideal-typical explanations that can help us to understand the observed variation and reduce the complexity of reality.

The purpose of this chapter is to analyze market making. This means to present the basic distinctions between ways of market making, and to discuss the different processes that lead to markets. A central component is to analyze how the different market forms that we have studied are made. Is there just one, or many different market-making processes? Over the last ten years the role of performativity has been popular, and highly discussed. The core idea is that the economic theory is the script for how a market should operate, and that real markets are made by following that script; an issue that we will discuss in this chapter.

We have already argued market making is an inherently social process, which grew out of other social relations, most notably networks. Market is not the first form of social interaction or economic coordination. Nonetheless, market making is a more general notion than organization of market or design of markets. We use the notion of "making" in a rather loose way, to acknowledge the obvious fact markets are made by people, which means we follow Berger and Luckmann, who say "the social world was made by men – and therefore, can be remade by them" (1991: 89). "Making" also refers to human activity, in contrast to the notion of "emergence," which has an evolutionary baggage (Sawyer 2001) and is tied to the idea there are natural laws governing the process.

This chapter begins with a short review of the existing literature on market making. We then turn to a discussion of perhaps the most central distinction regarding market making, namely, between markets that are the result of a decided order and those that have emerged as a result of mutual adjustment of actors. Then we briefly repeat the conditions of an ordered market, followed by the analysis of how different market forms are made. Making of markets is closely related to change of markets. To discuss market change will be another task of this chapter. Finally, we discuss how markets are controlled and maintained.

The Study of Market Making

Economists, as we have argued, see markets as natural, which means they are taken for granted and not really in need of being explained. Market making, according to the economic view, is a natural process that only becomes a problem if politicians or others tamper with the actors and their interest.

There are two leading ideas that have been used by economists to explain market making, one saying markets are naturally emerging social formations which, left to their own devices, result in equilibrium. This we call the idea of mutual adjustment, or spontaneous order. The other idea is that markets are the result of organized efforts by actors to intentionally create markets. We will look at each form, but the main ambition is to see how they are related.

Mutual Adjustment and Social Order

Market order as a result of mutual adjustment, which sometimes is called spontaneous order, is defined as a process in which the market is an unintended result of actors' activities. This general idea of grown and non-decided order was called "kosmos" by Hayek (1973: 38, 1988: 45; Weber 1978: 82–5), and "catallaxy" when applied to markets (Hayek 1976: 108–9). The term was used by Hayek to describe the order brought about by the mutual adjustment of many individual economies in the market. A catallaxy is thus the special kind of spontaneous order produced by the market through people acting within the rules of law of property, tort and contract" (Hayek 1976: 108–9). Adam Smith's, as well as Hayek's, view on markets is well known: "As every individual . . . intends only his own gain, and he is in this, as in many other cases, led by an invisible hand to promote and end which was not part of his intention (Smith 1981: 456). These sorts of invisible explanations of economic coordination in markets, "show that some overall pattern of design, which one would have thought had to be produced by an individual's or group's successful attempt to realize the pattern, instead was produced and maintained by a process that in no way had the overall pattern or design 'in mind'" (Nozick 1974: 18).

Spontaneous making of markets implies that neither the state nor any other form of organization participates in the making of markets. The formal idea of spontaneous making and order can be traced back to the Scottish Enlightenment and the writings of Adam Ferguson, Adam Smith, drawing on the ideas of Bernard Mandeville, and others. Later, Austrian school and evolutionary economists favored the idea of the market as the result of a natural process. Hayek's approach, claiming that markets grew out of barter, exchange, and trade (Hayek 1988: 42–3; Plattner 1989: 180), can be described as evolutionary economics (Hodgson 1996: 170–86). The market is the result of a process, which ends with a market in order. The actors involved may lack a conception of the market; it is an "unintended consequence." Evolutionary economists, furthermore, see institutions (rules) as the conceptual cornerstone of their explanations of how markets develop (Hodgson 1996: 34, 175–9), and agree that the rules of the market emerge on the basis of humans' impulse to survive (Hogdson 1996: 170–1).

Neoclassical economists (Bal and Goyla 1994; Spence 1979) have analyzed market making in a similar fashion to evolutionary economists, but more radically and less historically, and by using the originally Cartesian notion of economic actors who are like atoms or monads, each with a set of given preferences, whose activities in a natural process result in a market.

How could economists reach the conclusion that markets are natural? One reason is their tendency to be armchair anthropologists, presenting "fictitious" examples of exchange interaction, all assuming "economic man," such as "the transactions of the putative hunter, fisherman and boat-builder, or the man with plane and the two planks, or the two men with the basket of apples and the basket of nuts" (Veblen 1898: 382), though this, of course, is metaphorical reasoning.

Sociological schools of mutual adjustment

Spontaneous order, however, is an idea to which also some sociologist have subscribed. Harrison White presents an approach to producer markets that draws on the idea that order is the result of actors who are involved in social interaction, where there is a form of mutual adaptation (White 1992, 2002b: 266–83, 2008). The driving force in White's model of action, to remind the reader, is that identities are trigged by the need for control. The outcome of the market-building process, White says, is an unintended consequence of this "internal" orientation among producers (White 1993: 168). White explains how the producer market we discussed in chapter 6 emerges: "Each actual market emerged amid some network of other existing production market. When, in this context, some set of differentiated producers manages to establish itself as a set vis-à-vis an 'other side,' the amalgam of the outputs from this set becomes established as a product through concurrent cultural and technological rationalizations" (White 1993: 161).

The differentiation of the producers' products corresponds to the differentiation of their identities (White and Eccles 1987: 985; cf. Zuckerman 2000). Luhmann (1995) has presented a similar idea to White's, and stresses order as the result of a spontaneous process of egos coming together.

The population ecology school, on which many economic theories draw, uses biological metaphors to "explain" order. Members of this school see markets as somehow naturally emerging. To explain the existence of a market, this tradition argues that it is more efficient than other markets. Firms that successfully establish a niche are in competition, and there is an environment (ecology) in which firms operate. This tradition has had a strong impact on sociological thinking, and Harrison White has incorporated some of its ideas into his market theory.

The population ecology approach operates with three units: the population, its members, and the environment of the population (Boone, van Witteloostuijn, and Carroll 2002; Carroll 1985; Carroll and Swaminathan 2000; Greve 1996). To simplify, a market is made up of specimens of a species, and together they form the population. The dynamic component is selection, and the result of the system is assumed to reach an equilibrium (Hannan and Freeman 1977). This is to say that the very idea of equilibrium, which etymologically can be traced to states in nature, refers to the self-regulation of the system. The same logic applies to the specimens, the individual firms; some have adapted to the environment and thus are able to survive, whereas others succumb due to the competition. The approach emphasizes competition (Park 1936), and it has made contributions to the economic sociology of markets, for example, the idea of niche, that is, "the region of a resource space in which an entity can persist in the absence of competition" (Hannan, Carroll, and Polos 2003: 309; cf. White 1981). Those favoring this approach also acknowledge the simple but important idea that there are many different markets (e.g., Greve 1996: 55). Some population ecologists, however, seem to see markets as naturally evolving spontaneous orders, a view they share with other evolutionary thinkers such as Hayek (1988: 45). Moreover, the focus is often on only one side of the market, that is, the population of "producers" (e.g., Carroll and Swaminathan 2000). Additionally, population ecologists tend to separate markets according to density (Haveman 1993).

Thus, it is clear that population ecology has led to the development of some ideas that have been incorporated into economic sociology. However, as an independent school, it does not seem to add much to our understanding of different markets, or to what is going on inside a market or with the actors in these markets. We claim that the observed behavior of market actors, for example, why firms differ (Carroll 1993) or how firms take positions in the market (Greve 1996), as well as specialization and centralization (e.g., Boone, van Witteloostuijn, and Carroll 2002), must be understood in relation to the specific form of the market (cf. Simmel 1983; White 1992). Only then can researchers separate profoundly different processes and different competitive structures.

Mutual Adjustment Leads to Markets

How shall we understand the process of mutual adjustment, and how does it lead to markets? We have already stated several times in this book that economists take markets as given, and as a result the very process that leads to them becoming real is of less interest.

But since it is clear that markets simply do not emerge, we must also ask why we should bother at all with describing a process that "does not really happen in reality." There are two reasons for this. The first is pedagogical. Only by a detailed outline of the process of market making as a result of mutual adjustment, will we see what an approach that stresses organized market making is lacking. The second reason is that sociological researchers have neglected the early phase of market making, which is constitutive of the economic actors. To rectify this situation, we should look more closely at the market-making process.

Spontaneous market formation is divided into three phases: *orientation*, *contraction*, and *cohesion*. These time-phases are illustrated in figure 7.1. This outline is deliberately ideal-typical, and does not capture the depth and variation of real market-making processes. In contrast to the Cartesian-atomistic idea assumed in economic theories, we presented in chapter 2 an essentially social human being as the starting point for understanding the economy. Thus, our discussion starts with social beings, but whose relations and identities are unclear, and ends – if completed – with an ordered market with stable roles, values, identities, a defined offer, a specific market culture, and a way of getting to prices. Hence, the spontaneous process presented here assumes a starting point of actors who are already in the social world, and who do have some cultural knowledge of markets in one form or other.

The first phase, which we shall call *orientation*, assumes that actors have an "interest" in trading. Different actors begin to check out each other's "offers." What later comes to be valued is typically up for grabs and not decided in the early phase of the market process (cf. Smith 2007), in which we can talk of "orientation among actors" without them envisioning a market as the end state of the interaction. Actors have different interests – in terms of what they want to trade and whether they are interested in buying

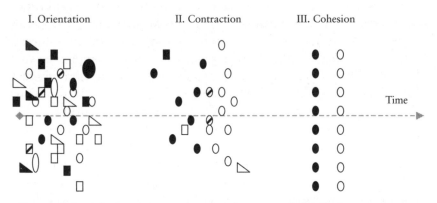

Figure 7.1 Actors in phases of market formation. Solid-fill shapes represent sellers and no-fill shapes represent buyers. Striped shapes indicate actors who are still undecided whether they are buyers or sellers. The different forms of the figures represent actors' different trading interests (different goods). Interests in only three broadly defined goods are illustrated here.

or selling – but their motives or preferences are also affected in this process of interaction; these have to be socially constructed and cannot be assumed. The participants in the process orient themselves more to those who display trading interests that are relevant for them. This means that a "buyer" looks at both those who want to sell and those who want to buy "the same thing" to see what they do. Actors begin to realize that there are others who have an interest in the buying and selling of offers that have some resemblance to each other. At this stage, actors do not know about the other actors in their new roles, or what they want. Information is neither free nor easy to obtain, as there is no central device that gathers, transmits, or sells information; it is not even clear what "market information" is. Actors' identities are in the process of formation, and old identities are changed as relations are negotiated, and, as a consequence, misunderstandings may be frequent. The toolbox (Swidler 1986) of the actors and the cognitive infrastructure available is largely made up of ideas of how other markets function, and how to behave in these. Some actors may bring their identities from other markets into this new setting. But a market cannot just be copied; it has to take root in the new institutional setting, which may imply other conditions of market making.

The next phase of market development, *contraction*, refers to actors and things being drawn together. This means that actors come together and begin to recognize what others want to trade. The turmoil of the "market coming into being" is noticeable in the instability of actors' identities. Economic actors set up business, or enter from already existing markets, but many may go out of business soon afterwards. However, it gradually becomes clear what can be done by actors, in the widest sense, and what cannot be done. Thus, those who have "deviant" interests have to drift away or become excluded from interaction. In this process, actors watch each other (cf. White 2002b), which is the way an actor may come to realize that "this is not for me," as his or her deviant offers or interests are not relevant in this particular pre-structure of a market. This becomes clear through gossip in the industry. More and more things are taken for granted in actors' social interaction;

and we may see this as a sign of the making of the culture of the market, which includes what to expect from those in the market, what to talk about and when, and how to do so. Actors will gradually be forced to decide whether they want to trade, and thus become part of what is under construction, or to stay outside it. As time goes by, market roles, "buyers," or "sellers," as well as actors' identities in correlation with these roles, begin to take a more stable form, at the same time as it becomes clearer what "the market" is all about. The contours of identities and relations can be discerned, but the uncertainty concerning what the actors "are" is still too great to see this as an ordered market, though it is a preamble of a market. One may say that we can observe traces of "embededdness in emerging cognitive market networks" (Kennedy 2008: 273), when actors perceive that relations begin to be established in the market. It is, thus, only with interaction over time that things become clearer. Yet another theoretical possibility is that sometimes we "never" get past the contraction phase so that we only have a continuous "preface" of a market; this may be the case in markets in which neither the actors nor the items become stabilized, which can be observed in industries exhibiting rapid technological development.

The final phase is called *cohesion*, which refers to an ordered market. Only in this phase does it become clear what is sold in the market, which hitherto has been "under discussion"; the market is capable of evaluating what is exchanged in the market. This cognitive-practical knowledge that market actors have reflects the fact that each market is characterized by "a shared frame of perception among its firms" (cf. Fiss and Kennedy 2008; White 2002b: 2). It is only on this assumption that we can talk of order or stability in the market. When a "market" reaches the phase of cohesion, it can be labeled or, in other words, be given a proper name. This phase means that not only has the first prerequisite of a market been met, namely, defining what the market is all about, that is, the market category, but also the second one of determining "how things are done in the market," and the third, "how prices are generated," are met.

In addition to these three phases, we may add a fourth phase, *crisis*. In this phase, markets are disrupted and radical change takes place, with order no longer prevailing. The phase that follows a crisis, however, is not orientation – because this is a phase that lacks a concrete market history – but contraction.

This example reflects the aspects of order that we have already discussed, as resulting from a spontaneous process. There are empirical examples of spontaneous making and shaping of markets, as well as examples of market differentiation, for instance, when new market segments are the result of innovation, advertising, and many other social processes, such as the new car market for "minivans" (Rosa, Porac, Runser-Spanjol, and Saxon 1999). Darr and Zer-Gutman (2007) have shown how a market was created between lawyers and brokers. The brokers offered the service of helping the lawyers with branding by offering information to journalists. Augustsson (2005) has studied the development of Internet media companies from their initial chaotic struggle, to figure out who they were and how to categorize themselves, to the making of well-defined markets. He shows how the process, from almost "amateurism" in the orientation phase to the development of several different markets, unfolded over several years. In this process, it is not possible to identify a "mastermind" who determined or organized the outcome.

The different phases of the spontaneous market-making process presented here are also useful for understanding organized market making. There is one exception, however: the orientation phase belongs only to spontaneous making. This is to say that organized making begins with contraction.

Organized Market Making

The second ideal-typical way in which markets come about is due to order in markets being made and maintained largely in an organized fashion, which Hayek (1973) calls "taxis." This making process is the result of organization when at least two actors come together and decide on the order of the market (cf. Ahrne and Brunsson 2008). It is, furthermore, possible to identify two ways of organizing the making of markets, called "state-governed market making" and "self-governed market making." Sociologists are likely to argue that markets are organized, embedded, and conditioned by a background of institutions.

Organized making of markets is probably more common than the process of mutual adjustment. It is characterized by actors interacting as "political" players, negotiating about the construction of the market. The idea of organized making has dominated the sociological literature on the making and change of markets (e.g., Bourdieu 2005; Fligstein 2001; Fligstein and Mara-Drita 1996), and we saw in chapter 3 that this idea has support in the historical literature. This ideal-typical form of making implies that the three prerequisites we have discussed essentially have to be solved prior to the time that the market is running. This also assumes that there are actors who have a reasonably clear idea of who they are and what they want, what the market is, and how it should work. This means that the fundamental problem of ambiguity must be resolved.

Organized making, as we have said, is defined as the process in which actors come together, directly or indirectly, to create a market by decision. At the beginning of such a process, at least two actors have some ideas concerning the market, what will be traded, and how it will operate, in addition to a reason "why" there should be a market. Based on this, they may attempt (Ahrne and Brunsson 2008: 49) to organize a market. This usually means that actors have a similar "conception of control" (Fligstein 2001). This process of organization normally involves many actors, including the state and actors from adjacent markets.

It is possible to identify two ideal-typical ways of coordinating markets, and they are separated by the involvement of the state or of state organizations: "state-governed market making" and "self-governed market making." In both cases we may talk of the organized making of markets, but in the latter case actors come together and create a market without direct state involvement. Moreover, in these two cases of market organization, actors who are directly affected and others who are indirectly affected may take part.

Thus, markets can be set up by different kinds of actors, including stakeholders (cf. Kochan and Rubinstein 2000), located inside and outside the market(s) in question. Steering is done not only by political means, but also through other systems of governance (Djelic and Quack 2007), as well as by economic capital. As organized making, and especially state-governed market making, is well known, we shall not discuss it in the same detail as spontaneous making.

State-governed market making

We have discussed how states can, by means of regulations, patents (Troy and Werle 2008), and taxation, block some markets, and make and facilitate others, and they may ban markets for religious, ethical, or distributional reasons. There are several examples in the sociological literature of what states in liberal economies can do to regulate markets. Bourdieu's (2005) study of the French housing market is one example, and the regulation of the US market for human eggs and sperm (Almeling 2007) is another. States can also control alternative avenues of trade, which potential actors may want to use, to avoid taxation, customs duties, or fees in the regulated market, which we saw in the case of the British Crown. State control of markets, such as the lottery market, may be imposed to increase tax revenues (Beckert and Lutter 2009), but state control or prohibitions may also result in markets. The donation and trading of human organs may also develop into grey or black markets (Healy 2006: 123–7). Today the modern state is always relevant, not least through its agencies that seek to prevent hindrance of competition and corruption, but this does not mean that all markets are regulated. What is the role of the state in market-making processes?

It is control of the "power" of states that enables actors to pursue their ends (cf. Korpi 1985). Stakeholders, such as property owners, unions, and others, may try to influence states to fashion markets in different ways. In this way, they turn the state into an arena of struggle. The idea that the support of a state or of any other meta-organization – such as an industry organization – makes it possible to construct markets has been stressed by the regulation theory (Boyer 1990) and political economy (Hall and Soskice 2001) approaches. The question of how markets are actually made, however, is not explicitly addressed in this literature.

Fligstein has discussed the institutional and cultural requirements of markets. An idea that Fligstein shares with others is the intimate connection between the state and market building. Fligstein's "market as politics" approach stresses the interplay in market construction between the state and, predominantly, organizations in what he, following Bourdieu, calls "fields" (Fligstein 2001, 2008; Fligstein and Mara-Drita 1996; Hellman 2007). According to Fligstein, markets that are in the formation process are characterized by a form of politics that resembles "social movements"; each firm that takes part is trying to impose its "conception of control," but they may also form coalitions (Fligstein 2001: 76). In this phase, which we have called contraction, "market actors" try to build institutions. The majority of institutions, however, are imported from adjacent markets. Also, many competitors enter from related markets (Fligstein 2001: 78). Eventually, a market comes to be ordered.

Self-governed market making

A state is not a necessary condition for either the existence or the making of a market. There is, as we have shown, much evidence suggesting that markets have evolved and existed without the support of a state, and despite state efforts to control markets. Various forms of illegal market (Ruggiero and South 1997) exemplify this. Moreover, states may even play an active part in illegal markets, such as when liberal markets for military equipment become politicized and embargos are implemented (Karp 1994).

Self-governed organized making of markets also begins with the contraction phase. In this case, a state – or a state-like organization – plays no direct role in how the market is constructed. It is therefore possible to talk of "self-regulated" markets (Gupta and Lad 1983; Mollgaard 1997), which may be an answer to the threat of regulation by the state. Self-governed organized making has many things in common with self-regulation, which is defined as "a regulatory process whereby an industry-level, as opposed to a government- or firm-level, organization (such as a trade association or a professional society) sets and enforces rules and standards relating to the conduct of firms in the industry" (Gupta and Lad 1983: 417). This is the case in some markets, such as the Chicago derivatives market (MacKenzie 2006; MacKenzie and Millo 2003). In other cases, the institutions of the market have been fashioned, as when the "big five accounting firms" withdrew from the professional association's training program and set up their own structure of trade (Garud, Hardy, and Maguire 2007; Greenwood and Suddaby 2006).

Simmel (1955: 147, 155–6) proposes collaboration among market members should occur, typically through business or industry organizations, which can be seen as modern examples of guilds, as was argued by Commons. This can mean that actors who share some interests come together and create the "rules of the game" – that is, formal institutions of the market – and thus meet the second prerequisite (cf. Ahrne and Brunsson 2008). This may include furthering the collective interest of, in some cases, only producers in a market (in relation to other markets or in relation to the other side of the market). Actors on one side of the market may, for example, decide on the right of entrance and conditions of trade, which, however, does not hinder fierce competition among market actors on the basis of price, quality, marketing, market share, and service or product development. Thus, the second prerequisite is met simultaneously with the first, namely, what is traded in the market.

There is a famous description of the construction of a market as a result of deliberate actions taken by actors without the direct help of, or hindrance from, a state, by Garcia-Parpet (2007). This is the story of how French strawberry farmers came together to set up a local market with the help of their association. There are yet other markets that have been created "outside" the state. The US diamond industry is one such example, and it has been shown that traders in this industry have "rejected state-created law" (Bernstein 1992: 115). Though we lack knowledge of how the diamond market was made, it cannot be understood unless its strong embeddedness in the Jewish community and the monopolistic tendencies in the rough diamond exploration market are brought into the analysis. This is a reasonable interpretation since a market has its own members (Merrill and Palyi 1938) who are introduced to the trading culture, and who have to follow the rules and regulations of the trading association (Marshall 1920: 256–8). Charles Smith (2007) describes two emerging markets, "sponsored word/phrase Internet search engine markets" and "equity option markets," that throw light on the process of market making. He shows that these markets are more or less performed to mimic various theoretical models of auction markets. Smith explains that the objects of trade, especially in the case of the "word/phrase" market, had to be determined in the process.

In reality, we will of course find many mixed forms of market making, in which governmental and non-governmental regulators and market actors make a market over time. Yuval Millo (2007) has described this in detail in an analysis of index-based derivatives. Millo shows how the making of financial derivatives, that is, "financial contracts that use market indices as their underlying 'assets'" (Millo 2007: 196), are not only common, but are also co-constructed by "regulators" and "producers" of these devices. Millo shows that the first step toward derivatives in the first market was that of derivates traded in the US, taken in 1851, when they were standardized. This facilitated trade. The ongoing negotiations, in which roles and products are changed and enacted, explain what the product is about. The products, in other words, are the result of organized efforts, but these efforts must be seen as a process, and not simply a decision that aims at implementing a single theory. These phases are summarized in table 7.1.

Performing Markets

Though we have already discussed the situation in which markets are performed based on a theory several times, this literature has

Table 7.1 Phases of spontaneous and organized market making. The empty box suggests that the spontaneous process is analytically and historically prior to organized market making.

Degree of order	Phases of market making	*Spontaneous Making*	*Organized Making*
"Chaos" "Order"	1. Orientation	Coming to grips with what is happening, and who one is, in the setting	
	2. Contraction	Watching and interacting with each other	Deciding together about what to do
	3. Cohesion	Ordered market	
[Chaos] Crisis/ change	4. Crisis/ change	(Back to phase 2, Contraction)	

had a large impact on the discussion of markets (Barry and Slater 2005; Callon 1998b; MacKenzie 2006; Miller 2002, 2005). The argument is that the construction of a market is mapped on an existing market model, the neoclassical market theory, which is used as a blueprint in the process of constructing or changing real markets. This organization may be done with or without the state playing a role. Callon says that his position "consists in maintaining that economics, in the broad sense of the term, performs, shapes and formats the economy, rather than observing how it functions" (1998a: 2). It is in this light clear that markets are organized, and not something that emerge spontaneously; Callon continues: "the market implies an organization, so that one has to talk of an organized market (and the possible multiplicity of forms of organization) in order to take into account the variety of calculative agencies and their distribution" (Callon 1998a: 3).

The idea of performativity has involved studying market formation processes in which actors come together and fashion an existing market, or make a new market. Economists play a key role in this process (Guala 2007). An interesting aspect of the performative perspective is that the economic profession is in focus. Social scientists should study the economic profession, since this profession has produced the knowledge that agents use when they perform the economy (Callon 1998a: 30). This means that sociological studies should generate "not a more complex homo economicus but the comprehension of his simplicity and poverty" (Callon 1998a: 50). Callon's main point is neither to enrich nor replace *homo economicus*. We should, instead, study how he comes about.

Callon stresses the central role that economic theory plays for markets. We have seen that the sociological literature, with the exception of White, has not really paid enough attention to the fact that there are different sorts of markets. The result is that sociologists have studied either producer markets or financial markets. Callon and his followers have only studied the markets that are organized in the way the neoclassical model assumes; they have not looked at the majority of markets that are producer markets. We should recall, however, that only a very small fraction of these markets has a history resembling what the performativity literature, with the exception of MacKenzie (2006) who also discusses counter-performativity, retells: first we have theory then we make markets accordingly. We clearly saw that the origins of the neoclassical theory, as developed by Walras and Marshall, are based on real markets. Marshall, for example, made the point that "stock exchanges ... are the pattern on which markets have been and are being formed for dealing with many kinds of produce which can be easily and exactly described, are portable and in general demand" (Marshall 1961: 328). Most markets are mapped on other markets, or have worked in a similar way to the neoclassical theory, even before this theory was properly formulated. The Chicago stock exchange, for example, is mapped on the New York stock exchange (Merrill and Palyi 1938: 561, n.1). We know, furthermore, that the London stock market was already by 1712 "active and organized" (Carruthers 1994: 170).

Making and Controlling Market Forms

We are now ready to formulate some ideas on how and when we can expect markets to be organized and when they are more likely to be the result of mutual adjustment. If markets seldom emerge naturally, can they be left to their own devices? After the financial crisis that hit the world in 2008, the answer for most people is no. Obviously, basic law and order must be maintained in all spheres of life, and there are specific laws that apply to the economy. The state must monitor all parts of social life, but what more specifically about markets? It must be clear we are dealing with two different things here; one is regulation of laws, access to markets, and the other is different forms of rules and competition, which are not the result of a political decision.

Politics often play a role in the market-making process (Bourdieu 2005; Fligstein 2001). This is, for example, the case in a contested market, such as housing markets, which in many European countries, at least, have been regulated. However, it is almost paradoxical that many economists assume markets to emerge naturally, and that the real market on which their model is based is probably the most organized. Alfred Marshall is clear about this: "The most highly organized exchanges are the Stock Exchanges" (1920: 256–7). Walras seems to agree: "The markets which are best organized from the competitive standpoint are those in which purchasers and sales are made by auction . . . This is the way business is done in the stock exchange, commercial markets, grain markets, fish markets, etc." (Walras 1954: 83–4).

We can assume that the combination of standard markets and switch-role markets, manifested in stock exchange markets, calls for a high degree of organization to be in order. All the prerequisites must essentially be solved by organization, and control and maintenance of this market must be organized.

Fixed-role markets, and especially if we are talking of status markets, cannot be completely ordered by organization. This is what we observe in producer markets, such as fashion garment markets. Product differentiation is part of the essence of competition in these markets (Chamberlin 1953), and it cannot be organized; if so, it stops being *competition*. Moreover, status, if it is not merely to be replaced with a decided rank order, must be the result of actors' – both sellers and buyers – decisions. We can, thus, expect some markets to be highly organized, whereas others must be less, or at least differently, organized.

Control of markets follows the same pattern. There are two aspects of control that we should separate, passive and active. Passive control refers to the law, and monitoring of general laws of society, including those pertaining to the economy and markets. Active control refers to the formatting of the market and its conditions, and there may be a zone in which this resembles change of markets.

Switch-role standard markets, such as a stock exchange, need much monitoring, whereas in other markets, in which status creates order, less monitoring is usually enforced. Merrill and Palyi (1938) say that the closer we get to the "perfect market," characterized by competition, the more organization and control we need. In this case, control is exerted over the listed firms, the members (those who trade), and by the government over the exchange. We may conclude that market competition is one form among many in which actors may coordinate their activities. The conflict of interest among actors in social life and in markets may drive them toward network relations or organizations within markets.

Change in Markets

How shall we account for change in markets? The idea of making and change are interconnected, but they are nonetheless distinctly different. Though most markets are stable over time (Burt 1988), this does not exclude change. Change is a matter of degree, and some change can always be observed (Djelic and Quack 2007: 163–8). Change in markets is usually considered radical change. A change in a market, in this sense, takes place as a result of external pressure – for example, regulations – but it can also be due to a market innovation by an entrepreneur (Schumpeter 2000), or organized by market actors in concert. Markets do change and new markets may be made because of human interaction, entrepreneurship, competition, and creativity (Schumpeter 2000; Stark 2009; Utterback and Abernathy 1975).

In this book we have seen also that entrepreneurs can make use of opportunities in markets or by being structurally positioned between markets (Burt 1992), so that they can see how to make use of their knowledge of conditions in different fields. It can be an actor who, after having spent time in one country, starts to import goods into another where this good is not yet introduced. To account for change and dynamics in markets, we must include both actors' interpretations and structural positioning; the notion of identity as a means of reflexivity as presented in this book is apt for this task.

Summary

This chapter has discussed how markets are made. We have employed the tools and the knowledge we presented in the first six chapters. We see that in contrast to the historical account of how markets were made, in chapter 3, the ideas presented here highlight the mutual adjustment process. This is for two reasons, first, because it is likely that markets do emerge as an unintended result of actors who mutually adjust to one another's behavior, and, second, because the idea of how actors are co-constructed in the process is left out of the existing research. We have suggested that organized market making is common, and that some markets need more organization to come into being than others. A sociological approach to spontaneous making must account for the mutual constitution and making of the market and market actors' identities. It is, of course, possible to discuss this further and make more detailed hypotheses (Aspers 2009a; Möllering 2009), and, obviously, much more can also be said on change in general, and how it relates to the dynamics of markets (White 2002b).

8

Conclusion and Future Research

This book aims at understanding and explaining markets. This is of interest and value to practitioners; however, the questions of the book are posed from a scientific perspective. We have referred to everyday notions, such as consumer market and market commodity, but the aim has been to account for these notions and to explain them using theoretical concepts. It is not the market practitioners who need abstract knowledge in the form of theory, but social scientists. And it is not necessary for a skilled salesperson to be able to present an account of the market, either to his fellow sellers or to the customers. This book assumes that actors involved in markets will benefit from knowing more about the market. Regulators, those who are critical of the markets, but also lay persons given the centrality of markets in contemporary social life, should have knowledge of markets.

We have in this book tried to go beyond the numerous texts that simply review research on markets. The main reason for this is the need to offer a remedy to the dismal situation: "The study of market behaviour is a major theme, if not the major theme, of economic science as we know it . . . Yet if we ask an elementary question – 'What is a market?' – we are given short shrift" (Hodgson 1988: 172). Throughout this book, we have elaborated on this question and presented an answer: a market is a social structure for the exchange of rights in which offers are evaluated and priced, and compete with one another.

In this final chapter we will briefly summarize the contents of this book. First, we identify what we know, and this serves the additional purpose of identifying the blind spots in the literature on markets. The book ends with some concluding remarks, a suggestion of how to study markets, and, finally, offers some ideas of what remains to be done.

Everyday Interaction and Markets

Markets are an integrated part of the lifeworld for most of us who populate the globe. Today, resources of various kinds that used to be shared by groups are tied to individuals, and have increasingly become measured in terms of money. Markets are gradually replacing other means of coordination, at the expense of networks, but also of hierarchies. It is when the value of efficiency and money maximization becomes the benchmark for markets and non-markets that we can speak of an economization of our everyday interactions.

Many sociologists have unfortunately accepted the economic view that the economy is an arena of rational action, instead of seeing it as an arena which is as social as any other, but with a different subject matter and style. The view presented in this book, in contrast, draws on the notion of identity and views emotions as integrated in human action. The incorporating of identity and emotions in a framework is one way to create a theoretical starting point for a sociological theory of economic action.

The line taken in this work is to connect the different identities that we as human beings are given and make in social life – including those in economic life – and recognize them as essential for our being. In this way, the connection of economic action to emotions, a view to which anyone who has been involved in real auctions can subscribe (cf. Smith 1989), is as prevalent as non-economic actions. This approach is not trapped in psychology, since the structural positioning of actors conditions their being. Furthermore, several authors have recently tried to integrate emotions (Barbalet 2001) in economic sociology (e.g., Bandelj 2009a; Berezin 2009; Illouz 2008).

Understanding and analytical reflection

Sociology has a special place in the social sciences, its role being to produce knowledge that is self-reflexive. Though all sciences aim at generating new knowledge, many have failed to incorporate the reflexive aspect of knowledge production. To be more specific: most sciences are interested in producing knowledge, but do not include the process of knowledge production itself in the theoretical production. Economics is perhaps the most salient example of this neglect. The impact of economic theory, as formalized knowledge, may have been greater in terms of affect on the world than in making us understand it. It is largely through the work of sociologists that we have better understood the way this body of knowledge has affected the economy (Callon 1998b; MacKenzie 2006), following the long tradition of sociology of knowledge that started with Marx. We should, however, not forget that early economists like Keynes were aware of the impact of economic reasoning: "the ideas of economists political philosophers, both when they are right and when they are wrong, are more powerful than is commonly understood" (Keynes 1973: 383).

Economic theory is about markets, and how they function, but an implicit idea is how they can function even better. The aim, we argue, should primarily be to offer tools for understanding markets. In doing this, we must connect with the lifeworld, but reflection calls for theoretical tools, since we cannot reflect with the same tools and concepts that we want to understand. We have in this book attempted to provide tools for abstraction and reflection.

This is a form of analytical reflection, which on the one hand takes its object of study – markets – apart and makes us understand them, and, on the other hand, reflects on the knowledge produced in this very process. What are the consequences of the knowledge produced?

What Do We Know?

The discussions in this book draw on sociological research on markets, but have also taken the knowledge generated by anthropologists, economic historians, economists, and geographers into account. This requires us to not reduce the market to a flow of goods and services, and to include also the institutions that make market transactions possible. This means to relate the market to its non-market culture, in terms of formal and informal institutions. And so we have concluded by studying how markets are related to other coordination forms, firms in the form of hierarchy, and networks.

A few things should be explicitly highlighted. This study has shown two aspects: there are indeed elements that unify all things we call markets, but we have also seen that there are different types of markets. Of these two, the last is much more controversial, especially since we have not tried to differentiate markets according to the goods traded in the markets, as economists have done. Below, we briefly list seven general points that sociological research has established about markets. This is not an exhaustive list of what we know of markets.

1. One insight that has been with us since the dawn of sociology is that markets are part of a larger whole. This idea was also a guiding viewpoint for the works of Parsons and Smelser (1956), whose attempts to develop an integrating theory are often forgotten.[1]
2. We have shown that though the market in its ideal-typical form is different from networks and hierarchical organizations, real markets tend to depend on networks and organizations. Many markets are organized, and networks are often needed to coordinate a market in the economy.
3. Markets are largely the result of organized efforts, but we should not forget that they also affect the identities of those who take part in the market making.
4. Sociologists have studied and clarified the connection between markets and values. The discussion of values includes the role

172

of politics and ideology. This has already been a leading theme in the works of Marx, Weber, and Simmel.

5. We have shown that there are many different forms of markets.
6. We have seen that it is the interest of economic actors to generate monopolies. The state often wants a perfect market, and consumers tend to prefer monopolistic competition in order to make distinctions.
7. The notion of identity is a more realistic notion than that of "economic man." Identity has explanatory power and relates the economy to the entire existence of human beings, including emotions.

How to Study Markets – Ask Seven Questions

Based on what we know, it is possible to outline an approach for studying what we do not know about markets. We do not have enough space to apply it in detail, but the set of questions we pose is of course also intended to guide those who want to study existing markets. The approach takes one individual market as its point of departure, but at the same time does not forget that markets are embedded in one another. The questions are posed in a practical order, not a logical or hierarchical order based on importance (as this depends on the research question).

1. What is the market about? (Prerequisite 1)
2. Is it a status or standard market?
3. Is it a switch-role or fixed-role market?
4. What are the institutional foundation and the rules of the market? (Prerequisite 2)
5. How are prices set in the market? (Prerequisite 3)
6. What constitutes the environment of the market?
7. Is the market the result of organized efforts, or is it a result of spontaneous processes of mutual adjustment of actors?

To address this set of questions is often a first step of empirical analysis in order to understand markets, regardless of the specific question(s) posed in a study.

What Remains To Be Done?

This book has surveyed the literature on markets, and it is thereby glaringly clear that there are many blind spots. Many sociological, not to mention other fields', texts concerning the market have not been included in this book. We have tried to focus on the core issues in markets. There are, of course, many others that study relevant aspects of markets; for overviews, see, for example, Aldrige (2005), Fligstein (2001), Fligstein and Dauter (2007), Lie (1997), Plattner (1989), Slater and Tonkiss (2001), and Swedberg (1994, 2003, 2005b).

Each blind spot should be turned into a field of research to further our knowledge of markets. Let us briefly mention them, and point at some concrete ways to improve the current state, in addition to simply calling for "more research." There are, however, a number of general issues and strategic concerns that are of paramount importance for the future of the field called sociology of the market.

The first point is the need for theory development. In this book, we have focused on theoretical progress made over the last 30 years of sociological market studies. Though, in the eighties and nineties, the application of neoclassical economics to sociological market studies was a stepping stone, it has gradually become a hindrance for original sociological contributions. Sociologists have largely tried to solve the same problems identified by economists by adding sociological flesh to "economic man" and markets. The straitjacket that economics has become for sociologists must be removed. A sociological alternative must also consider and question the assumption that so far has guided the majority of sociological research on markets. This may require a fundamental rethinking, in which many of our taken-for-granted assumptions may be questioned. Below, we list seven points, or areas of research, that are in need of additional research.

1. Essentially, economists assume reality to be an objectively existing entity separated from, and unaffected by, the knowl-

edge production of social scientists. Sociologists have begun to develop theories about this, but more could be done.

2. Economic sociologists have attempted to show that the actions of "economic man" are constrained and conditioned by social relations. However, few serious attempts have fundamentally replaced "economic man" with the social human being. This book has pointed at the notion of identity as one way to establish a truly social foundation of economic action.

3. The labor market is not a special form of market. The existing research on labor markets has made surprisingly little theoretical advancement. It has largely accepted the neoclassical market model. This book provides tools that could be used for analyzing labor markets too.

4. Global markets have not yet been analyzed to the extent they deserve by sociologists.

5. We have seen how sociologists studying the research of financial markets have been separated from those studying producer markets. However, neither of these strands of studies has paid enough attention to money. First, money is the means of transaction in almost all markets, but we know little of the effects of money on market transactions. To what extent is value affected by money as the means of measuring value? What role does money play in the case of extending markets into other spheres of life?

6. The lack of studies on, and tools for, understanding the relationship between markets and non-markets is another blind spot in the research on markets. Though all markets are embedded in the lifeworld, and the environment of a market is the arena of other markets in which it is embedded, there is in addition a non-market environment. How can we best understand communication and "exchange rates" between markets and social formations for valuation and evaluation outside of the economy?

7. Illegal markets are another field that is neglected. This would most likely drive research into other coordination forms, too, such as networks. Illegal markets are not only of

importance per se, but also for theoretical reasons. What differences do we observe, if any, when comparing illegal and legal markets?

Hence, this book ends with new questions. I hope that this will inspire others, too, to study markets.

Notes

I Introduction

1 It is important, theoretically, to realize the centrality of property rights, but it is equally important to empirically acknowledge that property rights do not have to be sustained by the state, as it appears to us today. In a clan society, the head of the family or the heads of the clan may decide on disputes of all kinds, including economic disputes. In New York, property law did not codify stock exchange transactions as commercial contracts until 1909 (Preda 2009: 61–2). Of course, trade existed prior to this, and the system had rules to enforce property rights, but without the interference of the state. Prior to the twentieth century, stock exchanges were essentially self-regulated, but monopolies granted by the state increased their legitimacy.
2 Competition is often missed in definitions of markets (Lindblom 2001), which makes it hard to draw a useful line between trade and market.
3 In a producer market for bicycles, different producers stand in a competitive relation since all want buyers to choose their products. In this case, competition is ongoing, and it is not definite, or tied to a specific customer. In the competition for an item in an auction there is only one winner.

2 Coordination in the Economy

1 Throughout the book, I have used the Oxford English Dictionary (online) as a reference for English-language etymologies.
2 The notion "man" or "economic man" will be used when referring to the idea of "man" as used in the neoclassical economics.
3 In the population ecology literature, which studies how populations of firms function in competitive environments, based on an idea taken from biology, the notion of survival is central (Carroll 1985; Greve 1996; Hannan and

Freeman 1977). This school also stresses the role of adaptation to the environment by human beings and their organizations.

4 If uncertainty is turned into risk, it is possible to assign probabilities to outcomes. To achieve probabilities, three conditions for means–ends relations must be met: "(1) similarity across cases; (2) similarity over time; and (3) sufficiently large numbers of past observations" (Guseva and Rona-Tas 2001: 626). Although the difference between the two is in some sense semantic, calculability is, needless to say, a precondition of prediction.

5 Sociograms are analytically separate from networks, as they are not reciprocal. That A wants to be friends with B does not even imply that B knows of A's existence.

6 Though Granovetter's study should be praised, the distinction between strong and weak ties misses the point that it is not necessarily the structural relation (how often and how close the actors are) that is the reason why they have the same information, but because they are in the same domain. This idea is included in Simmel's analysis.

3 Markets in Social Life

1 It has been argued, for example, that the abstract use of "market" is untranslatable into the language and context of ancient Greek or Latin (Finley 1973: 22).

2 Polanyi talks of a process of disembeddedness. The notion of embeddedness, in the original Polanyian sense, refers to how certain products, such as labor, were turned into commodities. This notion presumes that one can separate labor from other activities. From what we know, it is exactly this that must be questioned. Our argument is that social life was originally "religious." By this, we mean all activities were part of a larger whole, all of which was interpreted in what we would call religious terms today.

3 Although aspects of this approach are to be found in American pragmatism (Beckert 2009a), not even pragmatists like Mead have fully escaped the egological approach, at least if contrasted with Heidegger's approach. This means that, ontologically, a human being is studied as an atom (Malhotra 1987) also by many pragmatists.

4 Forms of Markets

1 Available at: <http://www.justice.gov/atr/public/guidelines/horiz_book/toc.html> (last accessed January 25, 2010).

2 Lying and trying to cheat is thus "part of the game." It is possible that this logic is also used in Western countries by people rooted in the bazaar economy, and is a potential cause of clashing business cultures.

5 Order out of Standard Offers

1 This is not to deny that some brokers may be more trustworthy, and it is certainly the case that a property broker who usually deals with top-end properties will also give less luxurious homes a flair. However, this "effect" will not last after the sale, and it is unlikely that it will affect the price to a large degree.

2 Monopoly is the situation in which there is only one seller, but the logic is not different from the monopsony, when there is only one buyer (such as when there is only a state-run military). For the sake of simplicity, we will only speak here about monopolies.

8 Conclusion and Future Research

1 David Stark, who refers to Olav Velthuis, argues that Parsons made a pact with the economists (Stark 2009: 7), which implied that economists study value and sociologists study values (the social structure in which economic actions are embedded). Though we agree that sociologists have not really studied values to the extent we should have, Parsons's (1956) own work contradicts this idea as the explanation for the sociological neglect of values.

References

Abolafia, Mitchel. 1996. *Making Markets*. Cambridge, MA: Harvard University Press.

Ahrne, Göran. 1994. *Social Organizations. Interaction Inside, Outside and Between Organizations*. London: Sage.

Ahrne, Göran and Nils Brunsson. 2008. *Meta-Organizations*. Cheltenham: Edward Elgar.

Akerlof, George. 1970. "The Market for 'Lemons': Quality Uncertainty and the Market Mechanism." *Quarterly Journal of Economics* 84: 488–500.

Akerlof, George and Rachel Kranton. 2000. "Economics and Identity." *Quarterly Journal of Economics* 105: 715–53.

Akerlof, George A. and Rachel E. Kranton. 2002. "Identity and Schooling: Some Lessons for the Economics of Education." *Journal of Economic Literature* 40: 1167–201.

Akerlof, George A. and Rachel E. Kranton. 2005. "Identity and the Economics of Organization." *Journal of Economic Perspectives* 19: 9–32.

Akerlof, George A. and Rachel E. Kranton. 2010. *Identity Economics: How Our Identities Shape Our Work, Wages, and Well-being*. Princeton, NJ: Princeton University Press.

Aldridge, Alan. 2005. *The Market*. Cambridge: Polity.

Almeling, Rene. 2007. "Selling Genes, Selling Gender: Egg Agencies, Sperm Banks, and the Medical Market in Genetic Material." *American Sociological Review* 72: 319–40.

Arrow, Kenneth. 1974. *The Limits of Organization*. New York: W.W. Norton & Company.

Aspers, Patrik. 2001. "A Market in Vogue, Fashion Photography in Sweden." *European Societies* 3: 1–22.

Aspers, Patrik. 2006. *Markets in Fashion, A Phenomenological Approach*. London: Routledge.

References

Aspers, Patrik. 2009a. *How Are Markets Made?* Cologne: Max Planck Institute for the Study of Society, Working Paper 3/09.

Aspers, Patrik. 2009b. "Knowledge and Value in Markets." *Theory and Society* 38: 111–31.

Aspers, Patrik. 2010. *Orderly Fashion: A Sociology of Markets*. Princeton, NJ: Princeton University Press.

Aspers, Patrik, Sebastain Kohl, Jesper Roine, and Philippe Wichard. 2008. "An Economic Sociological Look at Economics." *Economic Sociology: The European Electronic Newsletter* 9: 5–15.

Augustsson, Fredrik. 2005. *They Did It: The Formation of Interactive Media Production of Sweden*. Stockholm: National Institute for Working Life.

Azarian, Reza. 2003. *The General Sociology of Harrison White*. Stockholm: Department of Sociology, Stockholm University.

Backhouse, Roger. 1996. "Economics is a Historical Process." In S. Medema and W. Samuels, eds, *Foundations of Research in Economics: How Do Economists Do Science?* Cheltenham: Edward Elgar, pp. 7–17.

Baker, Wayne E. 1984. "The Social Structure of a National Securities Market." *The American Journal of Sociology* 89: 775–811.

Baker, Wayne E. 1990. "Market Networks and Corporate Behavior." *The American Journal of Sociology* 96: 589–625.

Baker, Wayne and Robert Faulkner. 1993. "The Social Organization of Conspiracy: Illegal Networks in the Heavy Electrical Equipment Industry." *American Sociological Review* 58: 837–60.

Baker, Wayne E., Robert R. Faulkner, and Gene A. Fisher. 1998. "Hazards of the Market: The Continuity and Dissolution of Interorganizational Market Relationships." *American Sociological Review* 63: 147–77.

Bal, Venkatesh and Sanjeev Goyla. 1994. "The Birth of a New Market." *The Economic Journal* 104: 282–90.

Bandelj, Nina. 2009a. "Emotions in Economic Action and Interaction." *Theory and Society* 38: 347–66.

Bandelj, Nina. 2009b. "The Global Economy as Instituted Process: The Case of Central and Eastern Europe." *American Sociological Review* 74: 128–49.

Barbalet, Jack. 2001. *Emotion, Social Theory, and Social Structure, A Macrosociological Approach*. Cambridge: Cambridge University Press.

Barry, Andrew and Don Slater. 2005. *The Technological Economy*. London: Routledge.

Beckert, Jens. 1996. "What is Sociological about Economic Sociology? Uncertainty and the Embeddedness of Economic Action." *Theory and Society* 25: 803–40.

Beckert, Jens. 2006. "The Ambivalent Role of Morality in Markets." In N. Stehr, C. Henning, and B. Weiler, eds, *The Moralization of the Markets*. ed. New Brunswick, NJ: Transaction Publishers, pp. 109–28.

References

Beckert, Jens. 2007. *The Great Transformation of Embeddedness: Karl Polanyi and the New Economic Sociology*. MPIfG Discussion Paper 07/1. Cologne: Max Planck Institute for the Study of Societies.

Beckert, Jens. 2009a. *Pragmatismus und wirtschaftliches Handeln*. MPIfG Working Paper 09/4. Cologne: Max Planck Institut für Gesellschaftsforschung.

Beckert, Jens. 2009b. "The Social Order of Markets." *Theory and Society* 38: 245–69.

Beckert, Jens and Mark Lutter. 2009. "The Inequality of Fair Play: Lottery Gambling and Social Stratification in Germany." *European Sociological Review* 25: 475–88.

Beckert, Jens and Jörg Rössel. 2004. "Reputation als Mechanismus der Reduktion von Ungewissheit am Kunstmarkt." *Kölner Zeitschrift für Soziologie und Sozialpsychologie* 56: 32–50.

Bell, Daniel. 1979. *The Cultural Contradictions of Capitalism*. London: Heinemann.

Benjamin, Walter. 2002. *The Arcades Project*. Cambridge, MA: Harvard University Press.

Berezin, Mabel. 2009. "Exploring Emotions and the Economy: New Contributions from Sociological Theory." *Theory and Society* 38: 335–46.

Berger, Peter and Thomas Luckmann. [1966] 1991. *The Social Construction of Reality: A Treatise in the Sociology of Knowledge*. London: Penguin Books.

Bernstein, Lisa. 1992. "Opting out of the Legal System: Extralegal Contractual Relations in the Diamond Industry." *The Journal of Legal Studies* 21: 115–57.

Beunza, Daniel and David Stark. 2003. "The Organization of Responsiveness: Innovation and Recovery in the Trading Rooms of Lower Manhattan." *Socio-Economic Review* 1: 135–64.

Birtwistle, Grete and Linda Shearer. 2001. "Consumer Preference of Five UK Fashion Retailers." *Journal of Fashion Marketing and Management* 5: 9–18.

Blaug, Mark. 1992. *The Methodology of Economics: How Economists Explain*. Cambridge: Cambridge University Press.

Boltanski, Luc and Laurent Thévenot. 2006. *On Justification, Economies of Worth*. Princeton, NJ: Princeton University Press.

Boone, Christophe, Arjen van Witteloostuijn, and Glenn R. Carroll. 2002. "Resource Distributions and Market Partitioning: Dutch Daily Newspapers, 1968 to 1994." *American Sociological Review* 67: 408–31.

Booth, William James. 1994. "Household and Market: On the Origins of Moral Economic Philosophy." *The Review of Politics* 56: 207–35.

Bourdieu, Pierre. 1977. *Outline of a Theory of Practice*. Cambridge: Cambridge University Press.

Bourdieu, Pierre. 1984. *Distinctions: A Social Critique of the Judgement of Taste*. Cambridge, MA: Harvard University Press.

Bourdieu, Pierre. 1990. *The Logic of Practice*. Cambridge: Polity.

References

Bourdieu, Pierre. 1996. *The Rules of Art, Genesis and Structure of the Literary Field*. Stanford, CA: Stanford University Press.

Bourdieu, Pierre. 2005. *The Social Structures of the Economy*. Cambridge: Polity.

Bowles, Samuel and Herbert Gintis. 2000. "Walrasian Economics in Retrospect." *The Quarterly Journal of Economics* 115: 1411–39.

Boyer, Robert. 1990. *The Regulation School: A Critical Introduction*. New York: Columbia University Press.

Braudel, Fernand. 1982. *Civilization and Capitalism 15th–18th Century, Volume II, The Wheels of Commerce*. London: Fontana Press.

Braudel, Fernand. 1992. *Civilization and Capitalism 15th–18th Century, Volume II, The Wheels of Commerce*. Berkeley, CA: University of California Press.

Britnell, R. H. 1978. "English Markets and Royal Administration before 1200." *The Economic History Review* 31: 183–96.

Brooks, Geoffrey. 1995. "Defining Market Boundaries." *Strategic Management Journal* 16: 535–49.

Brunsson, Nils, et al. 2000. *A World of Standards*. Oxford: Oxford University Press.

Burt, Ronald S. 1988. "The Stability of American Markets." *The American Journal of Sociology* 94: 356–95.

Burt, Ronald. 1992. *Structural Holes, The Social Structure of Competition*. Cambridge, MA: Harvard University Press.

Burt, Ronald S. and Debbie S. Carlton. 1989. "Another Look at the Network Boundaries of American Markets." *The American Journal of Sociology* 95: 723–53.

Calıskan, Koray and Michel Callon. 2009. "Economization, Part 1: Shifting Attention from the Economy Towards Processes of Economization." *Economy and Society* 38: 369–98.

Callon, Michel. 1998a. "Introduction: The Embeddedness of Economic Markets in Economics." in M. Callon, ed., *The Laws of the Market*, pp. 1–58.

Callon, Michel. 1998b. *The Laws of the Market*. Oxford: Blackwell.

Callon, Michel and Fabian Muniesa. 2005. "Economic Markets as Calculative Collective Devices." *Organization Studies* 26: 1229–50.

Callon, Michel, Yuval Millo, and Fabian Muniesa. 2007. *Market Devices*. Oxford: Blackwell.

Carroll, Glenn R. 1985. "Concentration and Specialization: Dynamics of Niche Width in Populations of Organizations." *The American Journal of Sociology* 90: 1262–83.

Carroll, Glenn R. 1993. "A Sociological View on Why Firms Differ." *Strategic Management Journal* 14: 237–49.

Carroll, Glenn R. and Anand Swaminathan. 2000. "Why the Microbrewery Movement? Organizational Dynamics of Resource Partitioning in the U.S. Brewing Industry." *The American Journal of Sociology* 106: 715–62.

Carruthers, Bruce. 1994. "*Homo Economicus* and *Homo Politicus*:

Non-Economic Rationality in the Early 18th Century London Stock Market." *Acta Sociologica* 37: 165–94.

Carruthers, Bruce. 2005. "The Sociology of Money and Credit." In N. Smelser and R. Swedberg, eds, *Handbook of Economic Sociology*. Princeton, NJ: Princeton University Press, pp. 354–74.

Carruthers, Bruce and Laura Ariovich. 2004. "The Sociology of Property Rights." *Annual Review of Sociology* 30: 23–46.

Chamberlin, Edward. 1948. *The Theory of Monopolistic Competition, A Re-orientation of the Theory of Value*. Cambridge, MA: Harvard University Press.

Chamberlin, Edward. 1953. "The Product as an Economic Variable." *Quarterly Journal of Economics* 67: 1–29.

Coase, R. H. 1937. "The Nature of the Firm." *Economica* 4: 386–405.

Coase, R. H. 1988. *The Firm, The Market, and The Law*. Chicago, IL: Chicago University Press.

Commons, John. 1909. "American Shoemakers, 1648–1895: A Sketch of Industrial Evolution." *The Quarterly Journal of Economics* 24: 39–84.

Dalton, George and Paul Bohannan. 1971. "Markets in Africa: Introduction." In G. Dalton, ed., *Economic Anthropology and Development, Essays on Tribal and Peasant Economies*. London: Basic Books, pp. 143–66.

Darr, Asaf. 2006. *Selling Technology, The Changing Shape of Sales in an Information Economy*. Ithaca, NY: Cornell University Press.

Darr, Asaf and Limor Zer-Gutman. 2007. "Lawyers, Public Relations and the Media: A Changing Barter Economy within a Community of Practice." *International Journal of the Legal Profession* 14: 215–35.

Djelic, Marie-Laure and Sigrid Quack. 2007. "Overcoming Path Dependency: Path Generation." *Theory and Society* 36: 161–86.

Dodd, Nigel. 2005. "Reinventing Monies in Europe." *Economy and Society* 34: 558–83.

Durkheim, Émile. 1984. *The Division of Labour in Society*. London: Macmillan.

Durkheim, Émile. 1992. *Suicide: a Study in Sociology*. London: Routledge.

Earl, Timothy. 2000. "Archeology, Property and Prehistory." *Annual Review of Anthropology* 29: 39–60.

Eighmy, Thomas H. 1972. "Rural Periodic Markets and the Extension of an Urban System: A Western Nigeria Example." *Economic Geography* 48: 299–315.

Emirbayer, Mustafa. 1997. "Manifesto for a Relational Sociology." *American Journal of Sociology* 103: 281–317.

Entwistle, Joanne. 2002. "The Aesthetic Economy: The Production of Value in the Field of Fashion Modeling." *Journal of Consumer Culture* 2: 317–40.

Entwistle, Joanne. 2009. *The Aesthetic Economy of Fashion: Markets and Value in Clothing and Modelling*. Oxford: Berg.

References

Etzioni, Amitai. 1988. *The Moral Dimension*. New York: The Free Press.

Faulkner, Robert. 1971. *Hollywood Studio Musicians, Their Work and Careers in the Recording Industry*. Chicago, IL: Aldine Atherton.

Faulkner, Robert. 1983. *Music on Demand. Composers and Careers in the Hollywood Film Industry*. New Brunswick, NJ: Transaction Books.

Faulkner, Robert R. and Andy B. Anderson. 1987. "Short-Term Projects and Emergent Careers: Evidence from Hollywood." *The American Journal of Sociology* 92: 879–909.

Favereau, Olivier, Olivier Biencourt, and Francois Eymard-Duvernay. 2002. "Where do Markets Come From? From (Quality) Conventions!" In Olivier Favereau and E. Lazega, eds, *Conventions and Structures in Economic Organization: Markets, Networks and Hierarchies*. Cheltenham: Edward Elgar, pp. 213–52.

Fevre, Ralph. 2003. *The New Sociology of Economic Behaviour*. London: Sage.

Fine, Ben and Ellen Leopold. 1993. *The World of Consumption*. London: Routledge.

Finley, Moses. 1973. *The Ancient Economy*. London: Chatto and Windus.

Fiss, Peer and Mark Kennedy. 2008. *Of Porkbellies and Professions: Market Framing and the Creation of Online Advertising Exchange*. Working Paper. Los Angeles, CA: University of Southern California.

Fligstein, Neil. 2001. *The Architecture of Markets, An Economic Sociology for the Twenty-First Century Capitalist Societies*. Princeton, NJ: Princeton University Press.

Fligstein, Neil. 2008. *Euroclash, The EU, European Identity, and the Future of Europe*. Oxford: Oxford University Press.

Fligstein, Neil and Luke Dauter. 2007. "The Sociology of Markets." *Annual Review of Sociology* 33: 105–28.

Fligstein, Neil and Iona Mara-Drita. 1996. "How to Make a Market: Reflections on the Attempt to Create a Single Market in the European Union." *The American Journal of Sociology* 102: 1–33.

Foucault, Michel. 2002. *The Order of Things: An Archaeology of the Human Sciences*. London: Routledge.

Fourcade, Marion. 2009. *Economists and Societies: Discipline and Profession in the United States, Britain and France, 1890s–1990s*. Princeton, NJ: Princeton University Press.

Gadamer, Hans Georg. 1990. *Wahrheit und Methode, Grundzüge einer philosophischen Hermeneutik, Band 1, Hermeneutik*. Tübingen: J.C.B. Mohr.

Gambetta, Diego. 1996. *The Sicilian Mafia: The Business of Private Protection*. Cambridge, MA: Harvard University Press.

Garcia-Parpet, Marie-France. 2007. "The Social Construction of a Perfect Market, The Strawberry Auction at Fontaines-en-Sologne." In D. MacKenzie, F. Muniesa, and L. Siu, eds, *Do Economists Make Markets? On the*

References

Performativity of Economics. Princeton, NJ: Princeton University Press, pp. 20–53.

Garud, Raghu, Cynthia Hardy, and Steve Maguire. 2007. "Institutional Entrepreneurship as Embedded Agency: An Introduction to the Special Issue." *Organization Studies* 28: 957–69.

Geertz, Clifford. 1963. *Peddlers and Princes, Social Change and Economic Modernization in Two Indonesian Towns.* Chicago, IL: Chicago University Press.

Geertz, Clifford. 1992. "The Bazaar Economy: Information and Search in Peasant Marketing." In M. Granovetter and R. Swedberg, eds, *The Sociology of Economic Life.* Boulder, CO: Westview Press, pp. 225–32.

Gemici, Kurtulus. 2008. "Karl Polanyi and the Antinomies of Embeddedness." *Socio-Economic Review* 6: 5–33.

Gereffi, Gary, John Humphrey, and Timothy Sturgeon. 2005. "The Governance of Global Value Chains." *Review of International Political Economy* 12: 78–104.

Glamann, Kristof. 1977. "The Changing Pattern of Trade." In E. E. Rich and C. H. Wilson, eds, *The Cambridge Economic History, Volume V, The Economic Organization of Early Modern Europe.* Cambridge: Cambridge University Press, pp. 185–289.

Goffman, Erving. 1968. *Stigma, Notes on the Management of Spoiled Identity.* Harmondsworth: Penguin Books.

Goffman, Erving. 1974. *Frame Analysis, An Essay on the Organization of Experience.* Cambridge, MA: Harvard University Press.

Granovetter, Mark. 1974. *Getting a Job, A Study of Contacts and Careers.* Cambridge, MA: Harvard University Press.

Granovetter, Mark. 1985. "Economic Action and Social Structure: The Problem of Embeddedness." *American Journal of Sociology* 91: 481–510.

Granovetter, Mark. 1992. "Economic Institutions as Social Framework for Analysis." *Acta Sociologica* 35: 3–11.

Granovetter, Mark. 2007. "The Social Construction of Corruption." In V. Nee and R. Swedberg, eds, *On Capitalism.* Stanford, CA: Stanford University Press, pp. 152–72.

Greenfeld, Liah. 2001. *The Spirit of Capitalism, Nationalism and Economic Growth.* Cambridge, MA: Harvard University Press.

Greenwood, Royston and Roy Suddaby. 2006. "Institutional Entrepreneurship in Mature Fields: The Big Five Accounting Firms." *Academy of Management Journal* 49: 27–48.

Greve, Henrich R. 1996. "Patterns of Competition: The Diffusion of a Market Position in Radio Broadcasting." *Administrative Science Quarterly* 41: 29–60.

Grimm, Jacob and Wilhelm Grimm. 1971. *Deutsches Wörterbuch.* Leipzig: Deutsche Forschungsgemeinschaft.

References

Gronow, Jukka. 2003. *Caviar with Champagne: Common Luxury and the Ideals of the Good Life in Stalin's Russia*. Oxfrod: Berg.

Guala, Francesco. 2007. "How To Do Things with Experimental Economics." In D. MacKenzie, F. Muniesa, and L. Siu, eds, *Do Economists Make Markets? On the Performativity of Economics*. Princeton, NJ: Princeton University Press, pp. 128–62.

Gupta, Anil K. and Lawrence J. Lad. 1983. "Industry Self-Regulation: An Economic, Organizational, and Political Analysis." *The Academy of Management Review* 8: 416–25.

Guseva, Alya and Akos Rona-Tas. 2001. "Uncertainty, Risk and Trust: Russian and American Credit Card Markets Compared." *American Sociological Review* 66: 623–46.

Habermas, Jürgen. 1984. *Theory of Communicative Action, Volume One, Reason and the Rationalization of Society*. Cambridge: Polity.

Hall, Peter and David Soskice. 2001. *Varieties of Capitalism, The Institutional Foundations of Comparative Advantages* Oxford: Oxford University Press.

Hann, Chris and Keith Hart. 2009. *Market and Society: The Great Society Today*. Cambridge: Cambridge University Press.

Hannan, Michael T. and John Freeman. 1977. "The Population Ecology of Organizations." *The American Journal of Sociology* 82: 929–64.

Hannan, Michael, Glenn Carroll, and Laszlo Polos. 2003. "The Organizational Niche." *Sociological Theory* 21: 309–40.

Harrington, Brooke. 2008. *Pop Finance: Investment Clubs and the New Investor Populism*. Princeton, NJ: Princeton University Press.

Hasselström, Anna. 2003. *On and Off the Trading Floor, An Inquiry into the Everyday Fashioning of Financial Market Knowledge*. Stockholm: Department of Social Anthropology, Stockholm University.

Hassoun, Jean-Pierre. 2005. "Emotions on the Trading Floor: Social and Symbolic Expressions." In K. Knorr Cetina and A. Preda, eds, *The Sociology of Financial Markets*. Oxford: Oxford University Press, pp. 102–20.

Hatch, Mary and Majken Schultz. 2004. *Organizational Identity, A Reader*. Oxford: Oxford University Press.

Hausman, Daniel. 1992. *The Inexact and Separate Science of Economics*. Cambridge: Cambridge University Press.

Haveman, Heather A. 1993. "Follow the Leader: Mimetic Isomorphism and Entry into New Markets." *Administrative Science Quarterly* 38: 593–627.

Hayek, Friedrich. 1945. "The Use of Knowledge in Society." *The American Economic Review* 35: 519–30.

Hayek, Friedrich. 1973. *Law, Legislation and Liberty, A New Statement of the Liberal Principles of Justice and Political Economy, Volume 1, Rules and Order*. Chicago, IL: University of Chicago Press.

References

Hayek, Friedrich. 1975. "The Pretence of Knowledge." *The Swedish Journal of Economics* 77: 433–42.

Hayek, Friedrich. 1976. *Law, Legislation and Liberty, A New Statement of the Liberal Principles of Justice and Political Economy, Volume 2, The Mirage of Social Justice.* Chicago, IL: University of Chicago Press.

Hayek, Friedrich. 1988. *The Collected Works of Friedrich August Hayek, Volume I, The Fatal Conceit, The Errors of Socialism.* London: Routledge.

Hayek, Friedrich. 1991. *The Road To Serfdom.* London: Routledge.

Healy, Kieran. 2006. *Last Best Gifts, Altruism and the Market for Human Blood and Organs.* Chicago, IL: Chicago University Press.

Hedeager, Lotte. 1994. "Warrior Economy and Trading Economy in Viking-Age Scandinavia." *Journal of European Archeology* 2: 130–47.

Heidegger, Martin. 2001a. *Einleitung in die Philosophie, Gesamtausgabe, II Abteilung: Vorlesungen, Band 27.* Frankfurt am Main: Vittorio Klostermann.

Heidegger, Martin. 2001b. *Sein und Zeit.* Tübingen: Max Niemeyer Verlag.

Hellman, Kai-Uwe. 2007. "Bewegung im Markt." *Berliner Journal für Soziologie* 17: 511–29.

Hirsch, Paul. 1992. "Processing Fads and Fashions: An Organization-Set Analysis of Cultural Industry Systems." In M. Granovetter and R. Swedberg, eds, *The Sociology of Economic Life.* Boulder, CO: Westview Press, pp. 363–83.

Hirschman, Albert. 1986. *Rival Views of Market Society and Other Essays.* New York: Elisabeth Sifton Books.

Hobbes, Thomas. 1968. *Leviathan.* London: Penguin Books.

Hogdson, Geoffrey. 1988. *Economics and Institution: A Manifesto for a Modern Institutional Economics.* Cambridge: Polity.

Hogdson, Geoffrey. 1996. *Economics and Evolution, Bringing Life Back into Economics.* Ann Arbor, MI: University of Michigan Press.

Hodgson, Geoffrey. 2007. "The Revival of Veblenian Institutional Economics." *Journal of Economic Issues* XLI: 325–40.

Holm, Petter. 2008. "Which Way is Up on Callon." In D. MacKenzie, F. Muniesa, and L. Siu, eds, *Do Economists Make Markets? On the Performativity of Economics.* Princeton, NJ: Princeton University Press, pp. 225–43.

Illouz, Eva. 2008. *Saving the Modern Soul. Therapy, Emotions, and the Culture of Self-Help.* Berkeley, CA: University of California Press.

Ingram, Paul and Peter Roberts. 2000. "Friendship among Competitors in the Sydney Hotel Industry." *American Journal of Sociology* 106: 342–87.

Jeggle, Christof. 2009. "Leinenherstellung und regionale Migration nach Münster / Westfalen von 1580 bis 1635." In D. Dahlmann and M. Schulte Beerbühl, eds, *Migration und Arbeitsmarkt vom 17. bis zum 20. Jahrhundert, Gesellschaft für Historische Migrationsforschung.* Essen: Klartext.

Karp, Aaron. 1994. "The Rise of Black and Gray Markets." *Annals of the American Academy of Political and Social Science* 535: 175–89.

References

Karpik, Lucien. 2010. *Valuing the Unique: The Economics of Singularities*. Princeton, NJ: Princeton University Press.

Katsenelinboigen, Aron. 1977. "Coloured Markets in the Soviet Union." *Soviet Studies* 29: 62–85.

Kawamura, Yuniya. 2004. *The Japanese Revolution in Paris Fashion*. Oxford: Berg.

Kennedy, Mark. 2005. "Behind the One-way Mirror: Refraction in the Construction of Product Market Categories." *Poetics* 33: 201–26.

Kennedy, Mark Thomas. 2008. "Getting Counted: Markets, Media, and Reality." *American Sociological Review* 73: 270–95.

Keynes, John Maynard. 1973. *The General Theory of Employment, Interest and Money*. London: Macmillan.

Kiely, Ray. 2007. *The New Political Economy of Development, Globalization, Imperialism, Hegemony*. New York: Palgrave Macmillan.

Kirman, Alan. 1991. "Market Organization and Individual Behavior: Evidence from Fish Markets." In J. Rauch and A. Casella, eds, *Network and Markets*. New York: Russel Sage Foundation, pp. 155–95.

Kirzner, Israel. 1973. *Competition and Entrepreneurship*. Chicago, IL: Chicago University Press.

Knight, Frank. 1921. *Risk, Uncertainty and Profit*. Boston, MA: Houghton Mifflin Company.

Knorr Cetina, Karin. 2005. "How Are Global Markets Global? The Architecture of a Flow World." In K. Knorr Cetina and A. Preda, eds, *The Sociology of Financial Markets*. Oxford: Oxford University Press, pp. 38–61.

Knorr Cetina, Karin and Urs Bruegger. 2002. "Global Microstructures: The Virtual Societies of Financial Markets." *American Journal of Sociology* 107: 905–50.

Knorringa, Peter. 1995. *Economics of Collaboration in Producer–Trader Relations, Transaction Regimes Between Markets and Hierarchy in the Agra Footwear Cluster*. Den Haag: Koninklijke Bibliotheek.

Kochan, Thomas and Saul Rubinstein. 2000. "Toward a Stakeholder Theory of the Firm: The Saturn Partnership." *Organization Science* 11: 367–86.

Korpi, Walter. 1983. *The Democratic Class Struggle*. London: Routledge & Kegan Paul.

Korpi, Walter. 1985. "Power Resources vs Action and Conflict: On Causal and Intentional Explanations in the Study of Power." *Sociological Theory* 3: 31–45.

Kregel, Jan. 1998. "Financial Markets and Economic Development: Myth and Institutional Reality." In K. Nielsen and B. Johansson, eds, *Institutions and Economic Change, New Perspectives on Markets, Firms and Technology*. Cheltenham: Edward Elgar, pp. 243–57.

Krippner, Greta R. 2001. "The Elusive Market: Embeddedness and the Paradigm of Economic Sociology." *Theory and Society* 30: 775–810.

References

Krishna, Vijay. 2009. *Auction Theory*. San Diego, CA: Academic Press.

Kuhn, Thomas. 1962. *The Structure of Scientific Revolutions*. Chicago, IL: Chicago University Press.

Lakatos, Imre. 1970. "Falsification and the Methodology of Scientific Research Program." In I. Lakatos and A. Musgrave, eds, *Criticism and the Growth of Knowledge*. Cambridge: Cambridge University Press, pp. 91–196.

Lie, John. 1997. "Sociology of Markets." *Annual Review of Sociology* 23: 241–60.

Lindblom, Charles. 2001. *The Market System: What It Is, How It Works, and What to Make of It*. New Haven, CT: Yale University Press.

Lipsey, Richard et al. 1990. *Economics*. New York: Harper & Row.

Luhmann, Niklas. 1981. *Gesellschaftsstruktur und Semantik, Studien zur Wissenssoziologie der modernen Gesellschaft, Band 2*. Frankfurt am Main: Suhrkamp.

Luhmann, Niklas. 1988. *Die Wirtschaft der Gesellschaft*. Frankfurt am Main: Suhrkamp.

Luhmann, Niklas. 1995. *Social Systems*. Stanford, CA: Stanford University Press.

Lury, Celia. 2004. *Brands: The Logos of the Global Economy*. London: Routledge.

Lynn, Freda, Joel Podolny, and Lin Tao. 2009. "A Sociological (De)Construction of the Relationship between Status and Quality." *American Journal of Sociology* 115: 755–804.

Macaulay, Stewart. 1963. "Non-contractual Relations in Business: A Preliminary Study." *American Sociological Review* 29: 55–67.

McCracken, Grant. 1988. *Culture and Consumption: New Approaches to the Symbolic Character of Consumer Goods and Activities*. Bloomington, IN: Indiana University Press.

MacKenzie, Donald. 2006. *An Engine, Not a Camera, How Financial Models Shape Markets*. Cambridge: Cambridge University Press.

MacKenzie, Donald. 2009. *Material Market: How Economic Agents are Constructed*. Oxford: Oxford University Press.

MacKenzie, Donald and Yuval Millo. 2003. "Constructing a Market, Performing Theory: The Historical Sociology of a Financial Derivatives Exchange." *The American Journal of Sociology* 109: 107–45.

MacKenzie, Donald, Fabian Muniesa, and Lucia Siu. 2007a. *Do Economists Make Markets, On the Performativity of Economics*. Princeton, NJ: Princeton University Press.

MacKenzie, Donald, Fabian Muniesa, and Lucia Siu. 2007b. "Introduction." In D. MacKenzie, F. Muniesa, and L. Siu, eds, *Do Economists Make Markets? On the Performativity of Economics*. Princeton, NJ: Princeton University Press, pp. 1–19.

Maitland, Frederic. 1907. *Doomsday Book and Beyond, Three Essays in the Early History of England*. Cambridge: Cambridge University Press.

References

Malhotra, Valerie. 1987. "A Comparison of Mead's 'Self' and Heidegger's 'Dasein': Toward a Regrounding of Social Psychology." *Human Studies* 10: 357–82.

Malinowski, Bronislaw. 1922. *Argonauts of the Western Pacific, An Account of Native Enterprise and Adventure in the Archipelagoes of Melanesian New Guinea.* London: Routledge.

Mandeville, Bernard. 1924. *The Fable of the Bees, or Private Vices, Publick Benefits.* Oxford: Oxford University Press.

Marshall, Alfred. 1896. *Elements of Economics, Being the First Volume of Elements of Economics.* London: Macmillan.

Marshall, Alfred. 1907. "The Social Possibilities of Economic Chivalry." *The Economic Journal* 17: 7 29.

Marshall, Alfred. 1920. *Industry and Trade, A Study of Industrial Technique and Business Organization; of Their Influences on the Conditions of Various Classes and Nations.* London: Macmillan.

Marshall, Alfred. 1961. *Principles of Economics, edited with annotations by C. W. Guillebaud,* 2 volumes. London: Macmillan.

Marx, Karl. 1978. "Capital." In R. Tucker, ed., *The Marx-Engels Reader.* New York: Norton, pp. 294–442.

Masschaele, James. 1992. "Market Rights in Thirteenth-Century England." *The English Historical Review* 107: 78–89.

Mauss, Marcel. 2002. *The Gift, The Form and Reason for Exchange in Archaic Societies.* London: Routledge.

Menger, Carl. 1994. "The General Theory of the Good." In I. Kirzner, ed., *Classics in Austrian Economics: A Sampling in the History of Tradition,* vol. I. London: William Pickering, pp. 37–90.

Merrill, Francis and Melchior Palyi. 1938. "The Stock Exchange and Social Control." *American Journal of Sociology* 43: 560–77.

Miller, Daniel. 1987. *Material Culture and Mass Consumption.* Oxford: Blackwell.

Miller, Daniel. 2002. "Turning Callon the Right Way up." *Economy and Society* 31: 218–33.

Miller, Daniel. 2005. "Reply to Michel Callon." *Economic Sociology, European Electronic Newsletter* 6: 3–13.

Miller, Daniel, Peter Jackson, Nigel Thrift, Beverly Holbrook, and Michael Rowlands. 1998. *Shopping, Place and Identity.* London: Routledge.

Millo, Yuval. 2007. "Making Things Deliverable: The Origin of Index-based Derivatives." In F. Muniesa, Y. Millo, and M. Callon, eds, *Market Devices.* Oxford: Blackwell, pp. 196–214.

Mises, Ludwig von. 1981. *Socialism: An Economic and Sociological Analysis.* Indianapolis, IN: Liberty Fund.

Möllering, Guido. 2006. *Trust: Reason, Routine, Reflexivity.* Oxford: Elsevier.

Möllering, Guido. 2009. *Market Constitution Processes: The Case of Solar*

Power Technology Markets. Paper presented at the 2009 EGOS Colloquium. Barcelona.

Mollgaard, H. Peter. 1997. "A Squeezer Round the Corner? Self-Regulation and Forward Markets." *The Economic Journal* 107: 104–12.

Mützel, Sophie. 2007. "Marktkonstitution durch narrativen Wettbewerb." *Berliner Journal für Soziologie* 17: 451–64.

Nee, Victor and Rebecca Matthews. 1996. "Market Transition and Societal Transformation in Reforming State Socialism." *Annual Review of Sociology* 22: 401–35.

Nee, Victor and Sonja Opper. 2006. "Economic Transformation in Post-Communist Societies." In J. Beckert and M. Zafirowski, eds, *International Encyclopedia of Economic Sociology.* London: Routledge, pp. 93–127.

Nelson, Richard. 2005. "Introduction." In R. Nelson, ed., *The Limits of Market Organization.* New York: Russel Sage Foundation, pp. 1–24.

Nelson, Richard R. and Sidney G. Winter. 2002. "Evolutionary Theorizing in Economics." *The Journal of Economic Perspectives* 16: 23–46.

Ng, Irene C. L. and Lu-Ming Tseng. 2008. "Learning to be Sociable: The Evolution of Homo Economicus." *American Journal of Economics and Sociology* 67: 265–86.

North, Douglass. 1990. "Institutions and Their Consequences for Economic Performance." In K. Cook and M. Levi, eds, *The Limits of Rationality.* Chicago, IL: Chicago University Press, pp. 383–401.

North, Douglass. 2003. "Markets." In J. Mokyr, ed., *The Oxford Encyclopedia of Economic History,* vol. 3. Oxford: Oxford University Press, pp. 432–9.

Nozick, Robert. 1974. *Anarchy, State, and Utopia.* New York: Basic Books.

Pareto, Vilfredo. 1935. *Mind and Society, A Treatise on General Sociology,* New York: Dover Publications.

Park, Robert Ezra. 1936. "Human Ecology." *The American Journal of Sociology* 42: 1–15.

Park, Siyoung. 1981. "Rural Development in Korea: The Role of Periodic Markets." *Economic Geography* 57: 113–26.

Parsons, Talcott. 1929. "'Capitalism' in Recent German Literature: Sombart and Weber (Concluded)." *The Journal of Political Economy* 37: 31–51.

Parsons, Talcott and Neil Smelser. 1956. *Economy and Society.* Glencoe, IL: The Free Press.

Phillips, Damon J. and Ezra W. Zuckerman. 2001. "Middle-Status Conformity: Theoretical Restatement and Empirical Demonstration in Two Markets." *The American Journal of Sociology* 107: 379–429.

Plattner, Stuart. 1989. "Markets and Marketplaces." In S. Plattner, ed., *Economic Anthropology.* Stanford, CA: Stanford University Press, pp. 171–208.

Plattner, Stuart. 1996. *High Art Down Home, An Economic Ethnography of a Local Art Market.* Chicago, IL: University of Chicago Press.

References

Podolny, Joel. 1993. "A Status-based Model of Market Competition." *American Journal of Sociology* 98: 829–72.

Podolny, Joel. 1994. "Market Uncertainty and the Social Character of Economic Exchange." *Administrative Science Quarterly* 39: 458–83.

Podolny, Joel. 2005. *Status Signals, A Sociological Study of Market Competition.* Princeton, NJ: Princeton University Press.

Podolny, Joel and Greta Hsu. 2003. "Quality, Exchange, and Knightian Uncertainty." *Research in Sociology of Organizations* 20: 77–103.

Polanyi, Karl. 1957a. "The Economy as Instituted Process." In K. Polanyi, C. Arensberg, and H. Pearson, eds, *Trade and Market in the Early Empires, Economies in History and Theory.* New York: The Free Press, pp. 243–69.

Polanyi, Karl. 1957b. *The Great Transformation.* Boston, MA: Beacon.

Polanyi, Karl. 1957c. "Marketless Trading in Hammurabi's Time." In K. Polanyi, C. Arensberg, and H. Pearson, eds, *Trade and Market in the Early Empires, Economies in History and Theory.* New York: The Free Press, pp. 12–26.

Popper, Carol, Will Bartlett, and Deborah Wilson. 1994. "Introduction." In C. Popper, W. Bartlett, D. Wilson, and J. Le Grand., eds, *Quasi Markets in the Welfare State: The Emerging Findings.* Bristol: SAUS.

Porac, Joseph and Howard Thomas. 1990. "Taxonomic Mental Models in Competitor Definition." *The Academy of Management Review* 5: 224–40.

Powell, Walter. 1990. "Neither Market nor Hierarchy: Network Forms of Organization." *Research in Organizational Behavior* 12: 295–356.

Power, Dominic and Johan Jansson. 2008. "Cyclical Clusters in Global Circuits: Overlapping Spaces and Furniture Industry Trade Fairs." *Economic Geography* 84: 423–48.

Preda, Alex. 2005. "Legitimacy and Status Groups in Financial Markets." *The British Journal of Sociology* 56: 451–7.

Preda, Alex. 2009. *Framing Finance.* Chicago, IL: Chicago University Press.

Quine, Willard. 1961. "Two Dogmas of Empiricism." In W. Quine, ed., *From a Logical Point of View.* Cambridge, MA: Harvard University Press.

Quine, Willard. 1964. *Word and Object.* Cambridge, MA: MIT Press.

Robbins, Lionel. 1935. *An Essay on the Nature and Significance of Economic Science.* London: Macmillan.

Rosa, José, Joseph Porac, Jelena Runser-Spanjol, and Michael Saxon. 1999. "Sociocognitive Dynamics in a Product Market." *Journal of Marketing* 63: 64–77.

Rosenberg, Alexander. 1992. *Economics – Mathematical Politics or Science of Diminishing Returns.* Chicago, IL: University of Chicago Press.

Ruggiero, Vincenzo and Nigel South. 1997. "The Late-Modern City as a Bazaar: Drug Markets, Illegal Enterprise and the 'Barricades'." *The British Journal of Sociology* 48: 54–70.

References

Samuelson, Paul. 1969. *Economics, An Introductory Analysis,* 6th edn. New York: McGraw Hill.

Sawyer, R. Keith. 2001. "Emergence in Sociology: Contemporary Philosophy of Mind and Some Implications for Sociological Theory." *The American Journal of Sociology* 107: 551–85.

Schmid, Hans Bernhard. 2005. *Wir-Intentionalität. Kritik des ontologischen Individualismus und Rekonstruktion der Gemeinschaft.* Freiburg/München: Verlag Karl Alber.

Schumpeter, Joseph. 1975. *Capitalism, Socialism and Democracy.* New York: Harper & Row.

Schumpeter, Joseph. 1981. *History of Economic Analysis.* London: Routledge.

Schumpeter, Joseph. 2000. "Entrepreneurship as Innovation." In R. Swedberg, ed., *Entrepreneurship, The Social Science View.* Oxford: Oxford University Press, pp. 51–75.

Simmel, Georg. 1923. *Soziologie, Untersuchungen über die Formen der Vergesellschaftung.* München and Leipzig: Duncker und Humblot.

Simmel, Georg. 1955. *Conflict & The Web of Group-Affiliations.* New York: The Free Press.

Simmel, Georg. 1964. *The Sociology of Georg Simmel.* New York: The Free Press.

Simmel, Georg. 1978. *The Philosophy of Money.* London: Routledge.

Simmel, Georg. 1983. *Soziologie, Untersuchungen über die Formen der Vergesellschaftung, Georg Simmel Gesammelte Werke, 2.* Berlin: Duncker und Humblot.

Simon, Herbert. 1955. "A Behavioral Model of Rational Choice." *The Quarterly Journal of Economics* 69: 99–118.

Sklair, Leslie. 1997. "Review Essay: The Nature and Significance of Economic Sociology." *Review of International Political Economy* 4: 239–47.

Skov, Lise. 2006. "The Role of Trade Fairs in the Global Fashion Business." *Current Sociology* 54: 764–83.

Skre, Dagfinn. 2007. "Towns and Markets, Kings and Central Places in South Western Scandinavia c. A.D. 800–950." In D. Skre, ed., *Kaupang in Skiringssal, Kaupang Excavation Project, Publication Series, Volume 1.* Aarhus: Aarhus University Press, pp. 445–70.

Slater, Don. 1997. *Consumer Culture and Modernity.* Cambridge: Polity.

Slater, Don and Fran Tonkiss. 2001. *Market Society, Markets and Modern Social Theory.* Cambridge: Polity.

Smelser, Neil and Richard Swedberg. 1994. *The Handbook of Economic Sociology.* Princeton, NJ: Princeton University Press.

Smith, Adam. 1981. *An Inquiry into the Nature and Causes of the Wealth of Nations.* Indianapolis, IN: Liberty Press.

Smith, Charles. 1981. *The Mind of the Market, A Study of Stock Market*

References

Philosophies, Their Use, and Their Implication. Totowa, NJ: Rowman and Littlefield.

Smith, Charles. 1989. *Auctions, The Social Construction of Value.* Berkeley, CA: University of California.

Smith, Charles. 2007. "Markets as Definitional Practices." *Canadian Journal of Sociology* 32: 1–39.

Southerton, Dave. 2001. "Consuming Kitchens: Taste, Context and Identity Formation." *Journal of Consumer Culture* 1: 179–204.

Spence, Michael. 1979. "Investment Strategy and Growth in a New Market." *The Bell Journal of Economics* 10: 1–19.

Spence, Michael. 2002. "Signaling in Retrospect and the Informational Structure of Markets." *The American Economic Review* 92: 434–59.

Stark, David. 2009. *The Sense of Dissonance: Accounts of Worth in Economic Life.* Princeton, NJ: Princeton University Press.

Stehr, Nico, Christoph Henning, and Bernd Weiler. 2006. *The Moralization of the Markets.* London: Transaction Press.

Stigler, George J. 1982. "Economics: the Imperial Science?" *The Scandinavian Journal of Economics* 86: 310–13.

Stigler, George and Robert Sherwin. 1985. "The Extent of the Market." *Journal of Law and Economics* 28: 555–85.

Stinchcombe, Arthur. 1992. "Bureaucratic and Craft Administration of Production: A Comparative Study." In M. Granovetter and R. Swedberg, eds, *The Sociology of Economic Life.* Boulder, CO: Westview Press, pp. 345–61.

Streeck, Wolfgang. 2005. "The Sociology of Labor Markets and Trade Unions." In N. Smelser and R. Swedberg, eds, *The Handbook of Economic Sociology*, 2nd edn. Princeton, NJ: Princeton University Press, pp. 254–83.

Swedberg, Richard. 1990. *Economics and Sociology. On Redefining Their Boundaries: Conversations with Economists and Sociologists.* Princeton, NJ: Princeton University Press.

Swedberg, Richard. 1994. "Markets as Social Structures." In N. Smelser and R. Swedberg, eds, *Handbook of Economic Sociology.* Princeton, NJ: Princeton University Press, pp. 255–82.

Swedberg, Richard. 1998. *Max Weber and the Idea of Economic Sociology.* Princeton, NJ: Princeton University Press.

Swedberg, Richard. 1999. *Orientation to Others and Social Mechanisms.* Stockholm: Stockholm University Department of Sociology. Working Papers in Social Mechanisms (2).

Swedberg, Richard. 2003. *Principles of Economic Sociology.* Princeton, NJ: Princeton University Press.

Swedberg, Richard. 2004. *Interest.* London: Open University Press.

Swedberg, Richard. 2005a. *Hope and Economic Development: The Case of 18th-Century Sweden.* Ithaca, NY: Cornell Universtity, CSES Working Paper Series (#28).

References

Swedberg, Richard. 2005b. "Markets in Society." In N. Smelser and R. Swedberg, eds, *Handbook of Economic Sociology*. Princeton, NJ: Princeton University Press, pp. 233–53.

Swedberg, Richard. 2005c. "Towards an Economic Sociology of Capitalism." *L'Année sociologique 55*: 419–50.

Swidler, Ann. 1986. "Culture in Action: Symbols and Strategies." *American Sociological Review 51*: 273–86.

Thompson, Grahame. 2003. *Between Hierarchies and Markets: The Logic and Limits of Network Forms of Organization*. Oxford: Oxford University Press.

Thompson, Homer and R. E. Wycherley. 1972. *The Agora of Athens: The Athenian Agora Volume 14*. Princeton, NJ: American School of Classical Studies at Athens.

Thurnwald, Richard. 1969. *Economics in Primitive Societies*. London: Oxford University Press.

Trigilia, Carlo. 2002. *Economic Sociology: State, Market, and Society in Modern Capitalism*. Oxford: Blackwell.

Troy, Irene and Raymund Werle. 2008. *Uncertainty and the Market for Patents*. Cologne: MPIfG Working Paper 2/08.

Utterback, James and William Abernathy. 1975. "A Dynamic Model of Process and Product Innovation." *Omega 3*: 639–56.

Uzzi, Brian. 1997. "Social Structure in Interfirm Networks: The Paradox of Embeddedness." *Administrative Science Quarterly 42*: 35–67.

Varian, Hal. 1996. "What Use is Economic Theory." In S. Medema and W. Samuels, eds, *Foundations of Research in Economics: How do Economists Do Economics?* Cheltenham: Edward Elgar, pp. 238–47.

Veblen, Thorstein. 1898. "Why is Economics Not an Evolutionary Science?" *Quarterly Journal of Economics 12/3*: 373–97.

Veblen, Thorstein. 1953. *The Theory of the Leisure Class, An Economic Study of Institutions*. New York: New American Library.

Velthuis, Olav. 2005. *Talking Prices, Symbolic Meanings of Prices on the Market for Contemporary Art*. Princeton, NJ: Princeton University Press.

Volckart, Oliver and Antje Mangels. 1999. "Are the Roots of the Modern Lex Mercatoria Really Medieval?" *Southern Economic Journal 65*: 427–50.

Walker, Donald. 1996. *Walras's Market Models*. Cambridge: Cambridge University Press.

Walras, Léon. [1926] 1954. *Elements of Pure Economics, or The Theory of Social Wealth*. London: George Allen and Unwin Ltd.

Warde, Alan. 1994. "Consumption, Identity-formation and Uncertainty." *Sociology 25*: 878–98.

Weber, Max. 1922. "Wirtschaft und Gesellschaft." In *Grundriss der Sozialökonomik, III Abteilung*. Tübingen: Verlag von J.C.B. Mohr.

Weber, Max. 1946. *From Max Weber: Essays in Sociology*. Ed. H. Gerth and C. Wright Mills. London: Routledge.

References

Weber, Max. [1904–5] 1968. *The Protestant Ethic and the Spirit of Capitalism*. London: Unwin University Books.

Weber, Max. [1921–2] 1978. *Economy and Society, An Outline of Interpretive Sociology*. Berkeley, CA: University of California Press.

Weber, Max. [1923] 1981. *General Economic History*. New Brunswick, NJ: Transaction Publishers.

Weber, Max. 1998. *The Agrarian Sociology of Ancient Civilization*. London: Verso.

Weber, Max. 2000. "Stock and Commodity Exchanges." *Theory and Society* 29: 305–38.

White, Harrison. 1970. *Chains of Opportunity, System Models of Mobility in Organizations*. Cambridge, MA: Harvard University Press.

White, Harrison. 1981. "Where do Markets Come From?" *The American Journal of Sociology* 87: 517–47.

White, Harrison. 1988. "Varieties of Markets." In B. Wellman and S. Berkowitz, eds, *Social Structures: A Network Approach*. Cambridge: Cambridge University Press, pp. 226–60.

White, Harrison. 1992. *Identity and Control, A Structural Theory of Social Action*. Princeton, NJ: Princeton University Press.

White, Harrison. 1993. "Markets in Production Networks." In R. Swedberg, ed., *Explorations in Economic Sociology*. New York: Russell Sage Foundation, pp. 161–75.

White, Harrison. 1995. "Social Networks Can Resolve Actor Paradoxes in Economics and in Psychology." *Journal of Institutional and Theoretical Economics* 151: 58–74.

White, Harrison. 2002a. "Markets and Firms: Notes Toward the Future of Economic Sociology." In M. Guillén, R. Collins, P. England, and M. Meyer, eds, *The New Economic Sociology, Developments in an Emerging Field*. New York: Russell Sage Foundation, pp. 129–47.

White, Harrison. 2002b. *Markets from Networks, Socioeconomic Models of Production*. Princeton, NJ: Princeton University Press.

White, Harrison. 2008. *Identity and Control, How Social Formations Emerge*, 2nd edn. Princeton, NJ: Princeton University Press.

White, Harrison and Robert Eccles. 1987. "Producers' Market." In J. Eatwell, et al., eds, *The New Palgrave: A Dictionary of Economic Theory and Doctrine*. London: Macmillan, pp. 984–6.

Williamson, Oliver E. 1975. *Markets and Hierarchies: Analysis and Antitrust Implications*. New York: Free Press.

Williamson, Oliver E. 1981. "The Economics of Organization: The Transaction Cost Approach." *The American Journal of Sociology* 87: 548–77.

Williamson, Oliver. 1991. "Comparative Economic Organization: The Analysis of Discrete Structural Alternatives." *Administrative Science Quarterly* 36: 269–96.

References

Withford, Josh. 2002. "Pragmatism and the Untenable Dualism of Means and Ends: Why Rational Choice Theory does not Deserve Paradigmatic Privilege." *Theory and Society* 31: 325–63.

Xenophon. 1970. *Xenophon's Socratic Discourse, An Interpetation of the Oeconomics by Leo Strauss*. South Bend, IN: St Augustine's Press.

Zelizer, Viviana A. 1979. *Morals and Markets. The Development of Life Insurance in the United States*. New York: Columbia University Press.

Zelizer, Viviana. 1981. "The Price and Value of Children: The Case of Children's Insurance." *The American Journal of Sociology* 86: 1036–56.

Zelizer, Viviana. 2005a. "Circuits Within Capitalism." In R. Swedberg and V. Nee, eds, *The Economic Sociology of Capitalism*. Princeton, NJ: Princeton University Press, pp. 289–322.

Zelizer, Viviana. 2005b. "Culture and Consumption." In N. Smelser and R. Swedberg., eds, *The Handbook of Economic Sociology*. Princeton, NJ: Princeton University Press, pp. 331–54.

Zelizer, Viviana A. 2005c. *The Purchase of Intimacy*. Princeton, NJ: Princeton University Press.

Zuckerman, Ezra W. 1999. "The Categorical Imperative: Securities Analysts and the Illegitimacy Discount." *The American Journal of Sociology* 104: 1398–438.

Zuckerman, Ezra W. 2000. "Focusing the Corporate Product: Securities Analysts and De-Diversification." *Administrative Science Quarterly* 45: 591–619.

Zuckerman, Ezra W., Tai-Young Kim, Kalinda Ukanwa, and James von Rittmann. 2003. "Robust Identities or Nonentities? Typecasting in the Feature-Film Labor Market." *The American Journal of Sociology* 108: 1018–74.